USING THE FORCE:
Star Wars and Catholicism

Anthony Digmann

Ad Majorem Dei Gloriam
Dyersville, Iowa

Nihil Obstat:
　　Rev. Richard L. Schaefer
　　Censor Deputatus

Imprimatur:
　　Most Rev. Michael O. Jackels
　　Archbishop of Dubuque

The *nihil obstat* and *imprimatur* are official declarations that a book or pamphlet is free of doctrinal or moral error. No implication is contained herein that those who granted the *nihil obstat* and *imprimatur* agree with its contents, opinions, or statements expressed.

© 2019 Anthony Digmann

All Rights Reserved. No part of this book may be reproduced or transmitted in any form or by any means, electronic or mechanical, including photocopying, recording, or by any information storage or retrieval system, without permission in writing from the publisher. For information, address *Ad Majorem Dei Gloriam*, LLC, 879 5th St SW, Dyersville, Iowa 52040.

Scripture texts in this work are taken from the *New American Bible, revised edition* © 2010, 1991, 1986, 1970 Confraternity of Christian Doctrine, Washington, D.C. and are used by permission of the copyright owner. All Rights Reserved. No part of the New American Bible may be reproduced in any form without permission in writing from the copyright owner.

This book has not been approved, endorsed, or licensed by Lucasfilm Ltd., The Walt Disney Company, or any other person or entity affiliated with Lucasfilm, Disney, *Star Wars*, or related properties.

Book and cover design by Anthony Digmann.

Cover images:
"Dark Rift" courtesy of NASA
"Stars and lasers" photo by Tobias Cornille on Unsplash

First edition
Published by *Ad Majorem Dei Gloriam* LLC
Dyersville, IA

ISBN-13: 978-1-718-11062-5

For the greater glory of God.

Above all, I thank God for life, truth, love, goodness, beauty, the Church, and our family of saints and angels, especially the Blessed Virgin Mary. Thanks to my parents for all of their love and guidance, and for introducing me to *Star Wars*. Abundant appreciation goes to my wife, Stephanie, and children for their patience and flexibility with my various endeavors, including writing this book. Thanks to Mark Hart, Fr. Richard Schaefer, and Dr. James Papandrea for their suggestions and help bringing this book to publication. Also, special thanks to the Catholic Jedi who offered critiques of the early manuscript: Jerry McGrane, Andrew Miller, Br. Craig Digmann, Chad Thomason, Fr. Noah Diehm, and Fr. Kyle Digmann. *Ad majorem Dei gloriam!*

Contents

TIMELINE OF CITED CANON SOURCES IX
INTRODUCTION XI
    PREREQUISITES & CANON... XIV

CHAPTER 1: USING THE FORCE 1
    OF FILM AND FAITH 2
    MASTERS OF EVANGELIZATION 4
    PREACHING BEYOND THE CHOIR 7
    KNIGHT OF REALITY 9
    EVERY ANALOGY HAS ITS LIMITS..................................10

CHAPTER 2: *STAR WARS* ORIGINS 13
    RESURRECTING MYTH..14
    MYTH MASTER AND APPRENTICE.................................19
    HERO'S JOURNEY 21
    SAMURAI, WESTERNS, AND NAZIS 26
    GEORGE'S VISION 30
    SUCCESSFULLY NAVIGATING AN ASTEROID FIELD 32
    DAWN OF AN EMPIRE 34

CHAPTER 3: WHAT THE FORCE IS NOT 43
    DUALISM..44

  Pantheism 50
  Gnosticism 52
  Person or Power 53

CHAPTER 4: THE NATURE OF THE FORCE 55

  Reverence 57
  Love 60
  Holy Spirit 63
  Mortis 64
  Mystery 65

CHAPTER 5: JEDI 67

  Jedi Charisms 67
  Commitment 71
  Prayer and Meditation 72
  Jedi Clergy 74
  Attachment 77
  Theological Virtues 79
  Human Virtues 82
  Holy-One Kenobi 84
  Grand Master 87

CHAPTER 6: SITH 91

  Rule of Two 92
  Evil Personified 95
  Corrupted Light, Darkness Is 98
  Feeling Like Sith 105
  Power Play 106

CHAPTER 7: ANAKIN SKYWALKER 113

  Prophecy 114
  Knight Fall 115
  Savior & Redemption 120

CHAPTER 8: LIFE, DEATH, AND AFTERLIFE 127

  Thy Will be Done 128

- Death & Afterlife 131
- Immortality 134
- Ghost Anakin 137

CHAPTER 9: FURTHER COMMONALITIES 141

- May the Force be with You 141
- The Force will be with You, Always..................... 142
- I Find Your Lack of Faith Disturbing.................... 142
- Intercessory Prayer.. 147
- Communion of Saints 148
- Self-Sacrifice 151
- Diversity and Inclusivity 152
- Respect for Nature... 153
- Overcoming Fear.. 154
- Temptation.. 156
- Corruption 157
- BC and BBY 160
- Canons.. 161

CHAPTER 10: PITFALLS OF *STAR WARS* 163

- Logical Inconsistencies 164
- Commanding the Force....................................... 166
- The Dark Side are They 168
- Salvation 169
- Relativism 170
- Pluralism 174
- Merely One Myth among Many 178
- Sexuality 180
- Eastern Religions and Occultism 182
- Fantasy Indulgence 184

CONCLUSION 189

- Connecting to the Sacred 190
- Heaven 191
- Assured Victory 192

  COMMISSION 193
  OUR LIGHTSABER 194
BIBLIOGRAPHY... 197
ABOUT THE AUTHOR.. 204

Timeline of Cited Canon Sources

BBY: Before the Battle of Yavin
ABY: After the Battle of Yavin

32 BBY	*Episode I: The Phantom Menace* (1999)
22 BBY	*Episode II: Attack of the Clones* (2002)
22-19 BBY	*The Clone Wars* (2008-2014) TV
21-17 BBY	*Catalyst: A Rogue One Novel* (2016)
19 BBY	*Dark Disciple* (2015) Novel
19 BBY	*Episode III: Revenge of the Sith* (2005)
18 BBY	*Ahsoka* (2016) Novel
14 BBY	*Lords of the Sith* (2015) Novel
14 BBY	*Tarkin* (2014) Novel
11 BBY-5 ABY	*Lost Stars* (2015) Novel
5-1 BBY	*Rebels* (2014-2018) TV
0 BBY	*Rogue One: A Star Wars Story* (2016)
0	*Episode IV: A New Hope* (1977)
0 ABY	*Heir to the Jedi* (2015) Novel
3 ABY	*Episode V: The Empire Strikes Back* (1980)
4 ABY	*Episode VI: Return of the Jedi* (1983)

4 ABY	*Aftermath* (2015) Novel
5 ABY	*Aftermath: Life Debt* (2016) Novel
5 ABY	*Aftermath: Empire's End* (2017) Novel
28 ABY	*Bloodline* (2016) Novel
34 ABY	*Episode VII: The Force Awakens* (2015)
34 ABY	*Episode VIII: The Last Jedi* (2017)

Introduction

"You've taken your first step into a larger world."
– Obi-Wan Kenobi (*A New Hope*)

I have no memory of life without *Star Wars*; it has always been there. I was born in 1982 and grew up watching the original trilogy on VHS tapes recorded from TV, replete with 1980s commercials. It was no surprise for me that Darth Vader was Luke Skywalker's father; I seem to have always known it. Several *Star Wars* themes captured my childhood mind in spectacular fashion: the quest of a young character and his/her subsequent maturity, exposure to exotic places and beings, interaction of a team of other characters (many with their own character arcs), chases, escapes, lightsaber duels, family ties and tensions, political intrigue, overall depth and immersion into another realm, good combating evil, and a mysterious spiritual power at work throughout the galaxy. I believe this special combination has cemented *Star Wars* as a cultural phenomenon spanning multiple generations and has allowed the franchise a unique place in American social, and even spiritual, consciousness.

I also have no memory of life without Catholicism, having been raised in a practicing Catholic home. In my late teen years, though, I questioned and very nearly rejected Catholicism. Like George Lucas, the creator of *Star Wars*, I wondered why there were so many religions in the world and which one, if any, was actually true.[1] At eighteen I recall deciding that I was not going to be Catholic simply because I was raised Catholic. If I was going to believe in something and give myself to it, I had to know that it was true. Consequently, I launched into a passionate study of the religions of the world. Eventually, I found myself returning whole-heartedly to Christianity and thereafter falling in love with Christ and the Catholic Church. This, in turn, led to a desire to know God more deeply and to share the truth I had discovered with others, which has become my career.

In my love for Christ and his Church, as well as my fandom for the ever-popular *Star Wars* franchise, I see an incredible opportunity to fuse *Star Wars* and Catholicism in a fun and productive way. Being an amalgamation of popular human myths spanning various eras, cultures, and religions, *Star Wars* has elements familiar to us all. As Dick Staub notes, "Christianity is a prevailing myth of Western culture; Star Wars is a prevailing myth of our popular culture."[2] Proficient in cultural myths, both J. R. R. Tolkien and C. S. Lewis came to describe Christianity as the "one true myth" that all other myths reflect. **I have discovered in**

Catholicism the real, historical fulfillment of what *Star Wars* and other human myths merely imitate in fantasy. Thus, *Star Wars* is an opening into popular culture through which we may evangelize.

After years of professional service in the Church, I feel that we fail far too often to reach those on the margins or who have little exposure to our faith. As I have deepened my theological and spiritual life over the years, I have also grown in my appreciation for *Star Wars*. In fact, I have discovered many of the things I love about being Catholic can also be found within *Star Wars*.

I believe that by exploring *Star Wars* through a Catholic lens, we may enjoy three practical advantages. First, we may rediscover truths of our faith from a new perspective and share them more effectively with an increasingly post-Christian culture. Furthermore, we can learn lessons from the "parables" of *Star Wars* lore, being inspired by the virtues and avoiding the pitfalls illuminated therein. Finally, since there are also areas of disagreement between a Christian worldview and that of *Star Wars*, we may also use the interaction of the two as an opportunity to better understand our faith through such differences—a very practical skill to develop in our interconnected world of diverse beliefs and values. **I intend this work to be a practical tool for fans, parents, clergy, teachers, catechists, and others to illustrate the connections between the mythology of the *Star Wars* franchise and the eternal truths and richness of Catholicism.** Let us seek to grow by exploring them together.

Anthony Digmann

Prerequisites & Canon

A few introductory items are in order. While a reader need not be steeped in *Star Wars* mythology in order to benefit from this book, it does assume that the reader is acquainted with the films. Some characters, locations, and events will be mentioned as basic *Star Wars* knowledge. In addition, this book explores other sources of information throughout *Star Wars* canon, and that brings us to another item: the topic of *Star Wars* canon.

George Lucas was the mastermind behind *Star Wars* and stood at the helm from its inception through October 30, 2012. On that date, Lucas sold Lucasfilm Ltd. (the parent company of *Star Wars*) to Disney, who has taken over management of all franchise property. This has ushered in an entirely new era for *Star Wars*. For example, Lucas produced six primary films for the franchise in thirty-five years; however, Lucasfilm under Disney has been, and plans to continue to be, much more prolific. They have produced a new movie each year, with several more planned for the future; produced two animated series, with more forthcoming; announced plans for live-action shows; produced numerous books, comics, and games based on the franchise; and they are likely to continue this indefinitely. This is a great time to be a fan of *Star Wars*.

In decades past, Star Wars took on a deep mythology, which expanded from the six films under Lucas's immediate direction to all kinds of books, games, videogames, comics, and eventually Lucas's exploration of an animated TV series begun in 2008, *The Clone Wars*. Within this "Expanded Universe" of material, there was minimal continuity regarding what could be done with a character or story—creators had considerable license in their storytelling. Lucas set the six films as the primary benchmark and allowed others to fill in gaps. At the time of Disney's acquisition, this all changed.

Under Disney's control, Lucasfilm took a much more organized and strict approach. The desire thereafter was to create continuity among the entire *Star Wars* franchise. As of April 25, 2014, the original and prequel trilogies, as well as the animated *The Clone Wars* series, were deemed the only official canon material, and the rest of the Expanded Universe material was rebranded as "Legends." This means the canon material offers the official storyline and timeline of the *Star Wars* universe. This was additionally necessary, because the Expanded Universe (now "Legends") had explored many events and characters chronologically following *Return of the Jedi*, which would make future exploration of that timeline by Lucasfilm under Disney difficult if they were forced to follow such storylines. Establishing this new canon gave Lucasfilm a clean slate and more creative potential, as well as solidifying the *Star Wars* collection of stories under an authoritative body who works to maintain continuity.

As a fan, I was excited to see this transpire. Prior to 2014, I was the kind of *Star Wars* fan who was "just interested in the movies." In the months preceding the release of *The Force Awakens*, I was convinced to try the two animated series: *The Clone Wars* and *Rebels*. I thoroughly enjoyed much of both shows. In fact, while Yoda remains my favorite *Star Wars* character of all time, mostly due to his sage-like qualities I suppose, my second favorite character has never appeared in a feature film. It is Anakin Skywalker's padawan, Ahsoka

Tano, who is featured in *The Clone Wars*, *Rebels*, and her own novel, *Ahsoka*. After watching *The Clone Wars* the first time, I concluded that it is not optional material for a serious *Star Wars* fan, because it fleshes out too much of the story and characters in the films to be ignored.

After Disney bought Lucasfilm, they announced a sudden end to *The Clone Wars*, even though it was incomplete, leaving fans without a conclusion to the storylines and characters under development. Wanting to continue following characters with whom I was enamored, I took another leap and launched into audiobooks and even a few graphic novels. The *Star Wars* audiobooks are second to none in production quality, with full dramatizations featuring voice actresses or actors playing the various parts in the novel, sound effects from the films, and *Star Wars* music from John Williams. They are like enjoying a long *Star Wars* movie without a picture. To date I have consumed over two dozen, which has enhanced my understanding of the *Star Wars* universe much more thoroughly and also augmented my experience of the films.

Due to what I have come to appreciate in the new canon, namely the animated and novel content, this book will also include information (and therefore spoilers) from those as well. I will attempt to offer fair warning, though, before spoiling a book or show, but the movies are fair game. These other sources offer much to enhance an understanding of *Star Wars* characters and their universe. Furthermore, they will prove valuable in order to more deeply explore connections between *Star Wars* and Catholicism. For context and orientation, a "Timeline of Cited Canon Sources" is included at the beginning of this book. For the critical *Star Wars* fan, I will also note that, since I was only interested in the films before Disney's acquisition of Lucasfilm, I know very little from Legends. Consequently, this book only includes material that is canon or ideas based on canon. Instead of, "May the Force be with you," I offer the greater blessing, "May the Lord be with you!"

---

[1] Bill Moyers, *The Mythology of Star Wars with George Lucas and Bill Moyers* (Public Affairs Television, Inc., 1999), https://vimeo.com/groups/183185/videos/38026023 (accessed 21 July 2017).

[2] Dick Staub, *Christian Wisdom of the Jedi Masters* (San Francisco: John Wiley & Sons, 2005), xx.

Chapter 1: Using the Force

"Use the Force, Luke. Let go, Luke."
– Obi-Wan Kenobi (*A New Hope*)

Star *Wars* has provoked a dialogue not only among fans, but also amidst religious scholars and has renewed mythological and religious themes in popular culture. The results have included people reading their religions and philosophies into the films, religious critiques, and even to fans around the world declaring Jedi to be their religion. While some of this activity is farce, *Star Wars* has such universal appeal because it reflects religious truth. It seems to be an inherent human trait to believe in God or a functional spiritual equivalent. The *Catechism of the Catholic Church* explains why: "God has placed [a desire for happiness] in the human heart in order to draw man to the One who alone can fulfill it."[1] We have an infinite longing for love, goodness, beauty, and truth that only God can fill, and *Star Wars* appeals to this hunger. This is especially true for those without a spiritual life, even though *Star Wars* can never fill such a void. Nevertheless, *Star Wars* can point to God. *Star Wars* also lends itself well to ecumenical discussion among fellow Christians, as well as other religions and philosophies, because every culture can find familiar elements in *Star Wars* mythology, and the franchise provides a non-threatening common ground and language.

Of Film and Faith

For Christians, George Lucas's myth may be religiously efficacious if connections between the films and faith are made apparent. *Star Wars* may serve as an inspirational story to open a Christian's mind to spirituality similarly to J. R. R. Tolkien's *The Lord of the Rings* and C. S. Lewis's *The Chronicles of Narnia*. Though *Star Wars* is not intentionally Christian, its deepest themes are richly Christian, including some details that are especially Catholic. Consider the following from Catholic writer, Steve Skojec:

> *Star* Wars presents us with a universe where good and evil are clearly distinguishable. Where nobility, virtue, and discipline matter. Where people care enough about doing what is right that they will fight against overwhelming odds in the hope of achieving it. Where rather than rabid individualism…a group of the sort of people…we might least expect to find success against such an overpowering force come together as a Tolkien-esque fellowship and do

exactly that. A story where even some of the most evil villains—individuals who fell into cruelty and darkness through vice and selfishness—can find redemption. In a word, *Star Wars* has a decidedly *Catholic* ethos.[2]

With similar appreciation for *Star Wars* from a Catholic perspective, film critic Steven Greydanus summarizes the original trilogy as, "The story of how evil is undone, neither by heroic violence, mystical power, nor Buddhist detachment, but by love: specifically, by filial piety, paternal attachment and moral conversion."[3] Literature and film professor, Roy M. Anker, identifies *Star Wars* as an "exultant fable of holy trust, apprenticeship, and pilgrimage that culminates in a resplendent vision of servanthood, reconciliation, and a winsome portrait of the new creation that awaits the cosmos."[4] He continues, "[It is] a riveting melodrama of redemption by love."[5]

Some Christians and academics find the fictional universe of *Star Wars* to be beneath them. However, we ought to recognize that the "child's play" of a fantasy like *Star Wars* is also good for adults. Caleb Grimes notes:

> Imagination is so much a part of who we are that children instinctively use it when they play. … Unfortunately, school, the pressures of growing up, and the hard issues that adults have to face, like paying bills, really threatens our re-learning to play.[6]

While play may seem frivolous, it is an essential component of being a happy, healthy human. Grimes encourages, "The *Star Wars* series is child's play, and it is adult's play. It stands as an encouragement to play."[7] It would do us well to recognize the value of imagination and fantasy, especially amidst worldly values to the contrary.

Masters of Evangelization

Our Catholic tradition has witnessed some masters of evangelization who offer guidance by their example of how we might use *Star Wars* to share our faith. St. John Bosco, for instance, was an Italian priest who worked among orphaned and neglected boys to ensure their spiritual formation, proper upbringing, and education. He understood that making a deep impact on his students meant he needed to get close to them first, to build a relationship with them, to care about them. He needed to understand and, to some degree, share their passions before they would be open to hear about his. One way he did this was through entertaining magic tricks. It has been said of him: "St. Bosco had pioneered the art of what is today called 'Gospel Magic,' using magic and other feats to attract attention and engage the youth."[8] Using *Star Wars* today as a staging point from which to launch into a discussion of Catholicism may be an example of such Gospel Magic.

Sean Fitzpatrick, Headmaster of Gregory the Great Academy, takes St. John Bosco's pedagogy to heart. He notices:

> Many things that draw the young are empowered by the dark side and, therefore, deserve no quarter as intrinsically perverse or

harmful. But *Star Wars* is not ranked among these. Though banal, it is, at bottom, benign, and its popularity is a powerful platform for a mutual jollity that can lead to a mutual affinity which is essential to any educational endeavor.[9]

Here Fitzpatrick suggests the need to be acclimated with those whom we serve in order to have a more profound effect. St. John Bosco concurred: "What is the secret of education? Love the things children love. ... A master who is seen in the master's chair is just a master and nothing more, but if he goes into recreation with the boys he becomes their brother."[10] Building on Bosco's testimony and witness, Fitzpatrick continues, "It is a paradoxical truth that silliness can make seriousness more achievable, and even things as specious as Star Wars can provide a bond for bigger and better things."[11] He further cautions: "Unless you love what your children love, they may find it difficult to love what you love someday."[12]

St. Paul is another excellent example of evangelization. He wrote, "I have become all things to all, to save at least some. All this I do for the sake of the gospel, so that I too may have a share in it" (1 Cor 9:22-23). He understood the necessity of building a relationship with others, on their terms, in order to lead them to Christ. When Paul was in Athens, he observed the people in order to relate the Gospel to what they already believed. This he found when he told the Athenians, "For as I walked around looking carefully at your shrines, I even discovered an altar inscribed, 'To an Unknown God.' What therefore you unknowingly worship, I proclaim to you" (Acts 17:23). He continued by sharing the Gospel of Jesus Christ as an alternative to their false gods. We ought to be so clever in our evangelization.

Indeed, it has been suggested that Paul was only able to speak in the Areopagus of Athens because he was familiar with Greek culture. Russell Dalton explains:

> He earned the right to speak to them by establishing his knowledge of their cultural texts. He quotes the philosopher Epimenides ("In him we live and move and have our being") and the poet Aratus ("For we too are his offspring"). ... Although Paul clearly did not agree with everything these authors wrote, he found insights in their writings that helped him reflect on his own faith and better communicate that faith to the people around him.[13]

The point here is that Paul first met his audience on common ground and with their language in order to evangelize them.

Pope St. John Paul II also understood the value of using contemporary means of communication, which he not only encouraged within the Church but also practiced himself. In his 1990 encyclical on missionary work, he referred to the importance of media in today's world and in the work of evangelization. After referring to the work of St. Paul above at the Areopagus in Athens (the place everyone went to share information) he recognized:

> The first Areopagus of the modern age is the *world of communications...* The means of social communication have become so important as to

be for many the chief means of information and education, of guidance and inspiration in their behavior as individuals, families and within society at large. In particular, the younger generation is growing up in a world conditioned by the mass media. To some degree perhaps this Areopagus has been neglected.[14]

Preaching Beyond the Choir

We are truly neglecting the means at our disposal to more effectively share our Catholic faith if we ignore the opportunities in popular media. These allow us to build rapport with others as St. John Bosco did, find common ground and common language as St. Paul did, and utilize the most effective forms of communication in our era as St. John Paul II encouraged us to do. **Star Wars is a tool we may use to evangelize those who know its mythology and to draw upon the similarities between it and our Catholic faith, as well as highlighting the differences between the two as additional learning opportunities.**

The importance of connecting with youth, and engaging them in topics of interest to them, is essential for evangelization. As George Lucas has repeatedly noted, *Star Wars* was intended for youth. Given Disney's primary marketing to such audiences, and their plans to continue to make *Star Wars* content into the foreseeable future, *Star Wars* is poised to remain a popular form of entertainment and influence for youth for decades to come. It has only grown stronger in the past 40 years, after all. Thus, learning to "speak" the mythology of *Star Wars* in a fun and engaging way is a minimal investment that may pay back dividends of evangelization success in the future.

It is easy and fun to draw connections between things in *Star Wars* and Catholicism with children, and it works just as well with adults. In fact, since *Star Wars* offers such a deep and rich mythology, adults can more fully appreciate the value of the comparisons. Considering how the popularity of the franchise has grown, even exploded in recent years, it is obvious adults are a significant portion of the fan base. Given that the 2015 release of *Episode 7: The Force Awakens* was the largest selling movie in domestic box office history, and that both *Rogue One: A Star Wars Story* (2016) and *Episode 8: The Last Jedi* (2017) were the best-sellers of their years, there is no doubt the popularity of *Star Wars* is as well established as ever. *Star Wars* is a force of evangelization (pun intended) we ignore to our own detriment.

While some fans of *Star Wars* are already religious, others are not. Russell W. Dalton has testified:

> Many people with little or no connection to organized religion have said that they use one or more of today's fantasy series as religious texts of sorts. They watch them or read them partly to help them reflect on the spiritual aspects of their own lives. For these reasons Christians who are about the spiritual life of others should explore these stories and not ignore them.[15]

Rather than preaching merely to the choir, we need to reach out to those on the margins, and we can thus harness the evangelization potential latent in *Star Wars*.

One example of the number of people in need of evangelization is illustrated by the international movement of those who have, seriously or whimsically, identified "Jedi" as their religious affiliation. A 2001 census revealed there are more Jedi (people who claim to "worship" the Force) in Scotland than Jews; similarly in Britain, Jedi numbered 390,000 or 0.7% of the population.[16] An e-mail campaign was responsible for encouraging people in England, Australia, and New Zealand to claim to be "Jedi" in the "other" category of the census.[17] Joshua Hays reports, "2011 census results identify 9,000 Jedi in Canada, more than 15,000 in the Czech Republic, and 65,000 in Australia."[18] Theologian, David Wilkinson, notes:

> The decline of traditional Christianity in the West has contributed to the search for alternatives. ... The popularity of *Star Wars* shows a deep hunger for spirituality within our Western society. It resonates with the desire to ask deep questions and find meaning and purpose in life.[19]

The fact that so many people hold no greater allegiance to an authentic religion than their fandom for *Star Wars* ought to give us pause.

Knight of Reality

Anyone interested in using *Star Wars* to share Catholicism ought to be familiar with the story of a special Jedi Knight. After decades exploring other religions and ideologies, including atheism, Sir Alec Guinness (the original Obi-Wan Kenobi) converted to

Catholicism and remained Catholic the latter half of his life.[20] While dressed as a Catholic priest in France for a 1954 movie he was filming, he encountered a boy who, convinced he was a real priest, cheerfully walked and talked with him.[21] Guinness commented:

> I reflected that a Church that could inspire such confidence in a child, making priests, even when unknown, so easily approachable, could not be as scheming or as creepy as so often made out. I began to shake off my long-taught, long-absorbed prejudices.[22]

A few years later Guinness's son, Matthew, contracted polio. While Alec was praying in a Catholic church he was fond of visiting, Alec told God he would convert if Matthew survived.[23] Following Matthew's recovery, the family became Catholic.[24] Nearing his death in 2000, Alec wrote: "If I have one regret…it would be that I didn't take the decision to become a Catholic in my early twenties. That would have sorted out a lot of my life and sweetened it."[25] This is a beautiful testimony to share with *Star Wars* fans as a way of bridging the fictional franchise with the genuine reality of our Catholic faith.

Every Analogy has its Limits

It is important to note that *Star Wars* is far from being a perfect representation of Catholic beliefs and values. Certainly, there are many areas in which the two align, and *Star Wars* serves as a great staging point from which to engage theology, philosophy, and morality. Nevertheless, *Star Wars* also contains a few elements that contrast with Catholic values. A further discussion of these is found in "Chapter 10: Pitfalls of *Star Wars*." Even these disparities, though, may be utilized to illustrate where *Star Wars* fails to reach the fullness of truth we enjoy as Catholics. This work intends to offer a Catholic interpretation of the *Star Wars* franchise, while also recognizing that other interpretations will exist, as with any artwork.

---

[1] *Catechism of the Catholic Church*, 2d ed. (Citta del Vaticano: Libreria Editrice Vaticana, 1997), § 1718.

[2] Steve Skojec, "Star Wars: Catholic Ethos, Universal Appeal," *One Peter Five* (17 December 2015) https://onepeterfive.com/star-wars-catholic-ethos-universal-appeal/ (accessed 24 March 2017).

[3] Steven D. Greydanus, "Is 'Star Wars' Gnostic?" *National Catholic Register* (29 December 2015) http://www.ncregister.com/daily-news/is-star-wars-gnostic (accessed 24 March 2017).

[4] Roy M. Anker, *Catching Light: Looking for God in the Movies* (Grand Rapids, MI: William B. Eerdmans Publishing Company, 2004), 222.

[5] Ibid.

[6] Caleb Grimes, *Star Wars Jesus: A Spiritual Commentary on the Reality of the Force* (Enumclaw, WA: WinePress Publishing, 2007), 51.

[7] Ibid.

[8] "St. John Bosco," *Catholic Online*, http://www.catholic.org/saints/saint.php?saint_id=63 (accessed 24 July 2017).

[9] Sean Fitzpatrick, "Use the Force: A Catholic Strategy for Star Wars," *Catholic Exchange* (21 December 2015) http://catholicexchange.com/use-the-force-a-catholic-strategy-for-star-wars (accessed 24 March 2017).

[10] Ibid.

[11] Ibid.

[12] Ibid.

[13] Russell W. Dalton, *Faith Journey Through Fantasy Lands: A Christian Dialogue with Harry Potter, Star Wars, and The Lord of the Rings* (Minneapolis: Augsburg Books, 2003), 3.

[14] John Paul II, Pope St., *Redemptoris Missio* (7 December 1990) http://w2.vatican.va/content/john-paul-ii/en/encyclicals/documents/hf_jp-ii_enc_07121990_redemptoris-missio.html (accessed 24 July 2017), 37b.

[15] Dalton, 2-3.

[16] Jenifer Johnston, "Jedi, Our Fourth Religion Thanks to the Pagans," *The Sunday Herald*, 28 March 2004, 6.

[17] Amanda Greene, "Faith & the Force," *Star News* (Wilmington, NC), 21 May 2005, 1D, 4D.

[18] Joshua Hays, *A True Hope: Jedi Perils and the Way of Jesus* (Macon, GA: Smyth & Helwys, 2015), 5.

[19] David Wilkinson, *The Power of the Force: the Spirituality of the Star Wars Films* (Oxford: Lion, 2000), 142.

[20] Alison Lesley, "How Obi-Wan Kenobi of 'Star Wars' Became a Devout Catholic" (14 December 2015) http://www.worldreligionnews.com/religion-news/christianity/how-obi-wan-kenobi-of-star-wars-became-a-devout-catholic (accessed 24 March 2017).

[21] Ibid.

[22] Ibid.

[23] Ibid.

[24] Ibid.

[25] Ibid.

Chapter 2: *Star Wars* Origins

"For over a thousand generations the Jedi Knights were the guardians of peace and justice in the Old Republic."
– Obi-Wan Kenobi (*A New Hope*)

The number of influences on *Star Wars* is vast, and George Lucas's way of combining them into his films in order to touch people so powerfully has been monumental. Literature and film professor, Roy M. Anker, compliments Lucas by recognizing that the only other "fiction maker to come up with anything at once so original and so authentic, so fully made and fresh, was J. R. R. Tolkien in his medieval-like saga of hobbits, orcs, and wizards."[1] Furthermore, George Lucas not only changed moviemaking in his day as a young writer, director, and producer with *Star Wars—*

his contribution impacted moviemaking both broadly and deeply thereafter. This chapter will explore the sources and inspirations behind *Star Wars*, Lucas's intentions for the films, and the overwhelming impact it has left on our culture.

Resurrecting Myth

An official documentary explains: "Born in Modesto, California, George Lucas grew up reading adventure stories and watching movie serials on television," such as *Buck Rogers* and *Flash Gordon*.[2] David Wilkinson reports: "When he was six years old, he had some kind of mystical experience. He later described it as, 'It centered around God, what is God, but more than that, what is reality? What is this?'"[3] As a youth, "His parents went to a Methodist church," which he disliked; "however, his housekeeper would take him with her to the German Lutheran church, where he liked the ritual."[4] As a college student at the University of Southern California, Lucas took an interest not only in filmmaking but also anthropology, philosophy, and mythology. Wilkinson continues: "He had long had a fascination with the great stories of human existence."[5] While working on his early films, such as *THX 1138* and *American Graffiti*, "[George] was talking about the fact that he would like to do a *Flash Gordon* kind of 1930s space opera," according to Gary Kurtz.[6] When asked why he wanted to pursue such a film, Lucas responded, "It's fun to make films for young people; it's a chance to sort of make an impression on them."[7] At the 40th anniversary panel of *Star Wars* Celebration in 2017, Lucas offered the following reflection:

Using the Force: *Star Wars* and Catholicism

> The idea was more I would like to make an action movie which is more like a Saturday morning serial that I enjoyed as a kid but imbue it with mythological, psychological motifs, because we don't have any more of those today.[8]

Part of the motivation for *Star Wars* was to bring back the positive elements of classical storytelling. In a 1999 interview with Bill Moyers, Lucas explained:

> I think the core issues that I'm dealing with are, if they were valid 2,000 years ago, they've got to still be valid today, even though they're not in fashion,…because I think the world we live in is more complex and I think that a lot of those moralities have gotten to be grayed to the point where they don't exist anymore, but those issues are still there.[9]

From a Christian perspective, Dick Staub agrees: "The lack of Yodas has resulted in such a loss for the next generation of aspiring Christians."[10] Describing the milieu of the 1970s, Mary Henderson notes, "When the first film in the *Star Wars* trilogy appeared in 1977, the ancient myths no longer seemed relevant for many people in this culture."[11] Enter *Star Wars*, which provided the mythology needed: "Here was a culture that needed new stories to inspire and instruct it—stories that would speak to modern concerns and at the same time offer some timeless wisdom."[12] Christianity was declining, and people's hearts were (and continue to be) longing for something spiritual and inspiring, yet not too demanding.

The religious implications are profound, because Americans' religious devotion is waning, and some are turning to *Star Wars* to fill some of this gap. Dick Staub observes:

> The original Star Wars trilogy appeared at a time when 95 percent of Americans said that they believed in God, but only 43 percent attended religious services. It is no wonder that these movies with their stories of rebirth and redemption and conquest of good over evil took on the power of myth. Values that had seemed lost to society were given new life in Star Wars: chivalry, heroism, nobility, and valor.[13]

Lucas reflects on this:

> I didn't want to invent a religion; I wanted to try to explain in a different way the religions that have already existed. ... I'm telling an old myth in a new way. ... This is again part of the globalization of the world we live in. ... The stories that I tell cut across all cultures and are seen all around the world.[14]

Lucas recognizes the importance of classical myths, especially their role in handing on the values essential to growing into adulthood. Seeing this in short supply in the 1970s, he sought to bring it back. Summarizing much of this, Lucas further explained at *Star Wars* Celebration in 2017:

> It's hard for people to realize, and I'm not supposed to say this, and I wasn't supposed to say it then, but it's a film for 12 year olds. ... It

was designed to be a film, like mythology, of this is what we stand for, you're about to enter the real world, you're 12 years old, you're going to go on into the big world, you're moving away from your parents being this big, center focus, you're probably scared, you don't know what's going to happen, and here's a little idea of some of the things you should pay attention to: friendships, honesty, trust, and doing the right thing, living on the light side, avoiding the dark side, those are things it was meant to do.[15]

Lucas has achieved what he set out to do. David Wilkinson—with a PhD in Astrophysics, turned Methodist minister, then PhD in theology, and current professor & principal of the Department of Theology and Religion at St. John's College of Durham University—reflects, "Within my own teenage experience those ideas began to resonate: there was more to life than just what we see; there is hope, and evil is real."[16] Much like Lucas, Wilkinson notes:

> I was not especially religious, but I was beginning to ask questions. ... *Star Wars* seemed to touch on these questions. It was good entertainment, but it was more than that. It never gave answers but it gave permission to ask the questions.[17]

As Lucas intended, putting big questions and issues in a mythological context makes them more palatable and less threatening. Wilkinson continues, "*Star Wars* and other movies allowed me to take those questions out of the seriousness of the reality of the situation and think about them in the freedom of the fantasy of fiction."[18]

Part of the problem with our culture is the religious gap, which allows *Star Wars* to come on the scene and fill in the role of religion in our contemporary world. "It's a sad thing to contemplate when a work of fiction all-but-supplants something as spiritually and historically significant as Christendom," observes Catholic blogger Steve Skojec.[19] He continues:

> But it also presents an opportunity: if a universally-loved phenomenon exists that crosses cultural and ideological boundaries, and draws heavily upon the very themes of good and evil, nobility, chivalry, and virtue that were once a fundamental part of the Christian West, it may actually represent a starting point for evangelization. I know it sounds crazy, but where an atheist will argue passionately with me about belief and doctrine, he is far more likely to agree with me about *Star Wars* canon. He is comfortable within the confines of a made up system of belief and history in exactly the way he is not in a real one. But there are elements of truth in the stories, elements that can be developed and expounded upon.[20]

Lucas intended for *Star Wars* to open reflective thought on both spiritual questions and contemporary issues. He reveals many of his intended key themes:

> *Star Wars* is made up of many themes, it's not just a single theme. One is our relationship to machines, which are fearful but as also benign.

… The issues of friendship and your obligation to your fellow man and to other people that are around you. That you have control over your destiny, that you have a destiny.[21]

Myth Master and Apprentice

Leo Braudy tells us: "With his galactic fairytale, Lucas hoped to reinvent a classic genre" built on what has become known as the "monomyth" or "hero's journey."[22] Lucas found much of his inspiration from mythologist Joseph Campbell (who was raised Catholic[23]) and his book, *The Hero with a Thousand Faces*, among others. According to Braudy, cultural historian and English/literature professor at USC, "What Campbell was interested in was to see the connections between myths, the myths of different cultures, to try to find out what were the threads that tied all of these very disparate cultures together."[24] In Lucas's own words, "I did research to try to distill everything down into motifs that would be universal."[25] He continues, "I attribute most of the success [of *Star Wars*] to the psychological underpinning which had been around for thousands of years, and that people still react the same way to the stories as they always have."[26] According to Bill Moyers, "Joseph Campbell said to me the best student he ever had was George Lucas."[27]

In essence, George Lucas built his plot and characters for *Star Wars* on classic myths and legends from all around the world, both ancient and more recent, to find the basic patterns that made stories classics. This included "such epics as *The Odyssey, Beowulf,* and *The Legend of King Arthur.*"[28] "I'm telling an old myth in a new way, that's how you pass down the meat and potatoes of your society to the next generation," Lucas told Bill Moyers in a 1999 interview.[29] "I consciously set about to recreate myths and the classic mythological motifs. ... What these films deal with is the fact that we all have good and evil inside of us and that we can choose which way we want the balance to go," Lucas continued.[30]

Lucas's efforts to use myth, religion, and philosophy in an epic story have been compared to J. R. R. Tolkien's *The Lord of the Rings* and C. S. Lewis's *The Chronicles of Narnia*,[31] yet Lucas did not limit himself to purely Christian influence. He wanted to create a modern myth with roots in the ancient myths of all cultures, and his sources include not only epics and myths but also stories from religions. Lucas explains:

> There's again a mixture of all kinds of mythology and religious beliefs that have been amalgamated into the movie, and I've tried to take the ideas that seem to cut across the most cultures, because I'm fascinated by that and I think that's one of the things that I really got from Joe Campbell.[32]

Lucas's success with *Star Wars* is largely due to his ability to tap into the common threads of popular stories shared by many cultures in varying epochs.

Lucas discussed the universal influences on his work in more specific ways as well. For example, in order to design Darth Maul, Lucas was inspired by images of personifications of evil from many cultures. He explains, "We went back into representations of evil, not only the Christian but also the Hindu and Greek mythology and other religious icons, and obviously designed our own character out of that."[33]

Certainly, *Star Wars* contains reflections of Taoism, Buddhism, and Hinduism, but it is primarily a Western construct, and is *de facto* primarily influenced by Judeo-Christian values. Roy Anker confirms, "Lucas takes elements from other world religions; but the central terms and structure of his story, as well as his verbal and visual language…suggest that Lucas's God in large part resembles the one depicted in Judaism and Christianity."[34] The Catholic/Christian elements of these will be explored in subsequent chapters, but it is valuable to recognize the broad cultural influences behind *Star Wars* and thus its international appeal.

Hero's Journey

As Lucas coalesced his study of popular myths from various cultures and religions across the globe, he found a core of character archetypes as well as a common plotline in the hero's journey. Joseph Campbell describes this in incredible detail, with multiple potential variations to the core stages of the quest. For our purposes, a simpler explanation may prove most helpful. In splendid three-part summary, Mary Henderson writes:

> First, the hero must *separate* [what Campbell calls 'Departure'] from the ordinary world of his or her life up to the point at which the story begins; then, in the new world through which the journey takes place, the hero must undergo a series of trials and must overcome many obstacles in order to achieve an *initiation* into

ways of being hitherto unknown; finally, the hero *returns* to share what he or she has learned with others.[35]

Lucas's original script for *Star Wars* was too big, so he cut it into three acts to make the original trilogy. As a result, it divides nicely to have *A New Hope* be the calling and departure, *The Empire Strikes Back* function as the trials, and *Return of the Jedi* represent the hero's return.[36] However, Lucas had to start with one successful film in order for the rest to see the light of day. *A New Hope*, and each of the films thereafter, also needed to include elements of these three main phases in their individual plotlines in order to stand alone. Therefore it is true that both the overall trilogy represents the phases in a broader sense, while each individual film also contains the basic three-part format, thereby adding depth to the storytelling process.

For the purposes of illustrating the phases of the hero's journey, we will be considering *A New Hope* almost exclusively. Obviously the hero's journey revolves primarily around Luke Skywalker, whose journey "transforms him from a rebellious and impatient teenager, itching for adventure, into a grown-up hero who has confronted his strengths and weaknesses and found the power to help save the world," writes Mary Henderson.[37] However, one of the beautiful elements of *Star Wars* is its depth, which includes the fact that more than one hero's journey is commencing simultaneously. Just as we see in real life, many people are undergoing this three-part transformation process at varying stages and ages. Henderson explains, "Part of the joy and fascination of this particular myth is that it is full of heroes sometimes found in the most unlikely places. Several of the main characters set off on a journey, encounter trials, and return profoundly changed."[38] In the original trilogy, for instance, we witness profound growth and change for Leia Organa, Han Solo, Lando Calrissian, and even Darth Vader. James Papandrea expounds:

> Although Luke Skywalker is the primary hero of the original three films, it is really a team effort. All of the main characters go through the hero's journey. Han Solo is the unbeliever who is converted, and he has his own death and resurrection when he is frozen in carbonite. Luke goes through a death and resurrection when he's pulled under the sludge in the garbage compactor. Leia is enslaved by Jabba the Hut, but she's the one who kills him… They all go through their ordeals, and they are all on a path toward salvation.[39]

Continuing with the hero's journey, we notice that heroes are often either of great or humble origins, experience a "call to adventure," and subsequently deny that call. In Luke's case, he appears a humble farm boy from a backwater nowhere (though we later learn the significance of his lineage, thereby giving him both qualities at once and additional appeal); he experiences the calling by Obi-Wan to study the ways of the Force to become a Jedi; and he denies it. Anker notices, "Tatooine is the equivalent of the biblical Galilee, Jesus' own obscure home territory, and by the end of the film Luke Skywalker will emerge, given the sacrifice he offers, as something of a Christ figure."[40] Interestingly,

Henderson notes that C-3PO "prophetically" calls Luke, "Sir Luke," in their early conversation to reveal his knightly destiny, which—though Luke denies both destiny and title at the outset—he will nonetheless come to achieve by the end of the trilogy.[41]

At the next stage, the hero-to-be encounters "supernatural aid." Campbell explains, "The first encounter of the hero-journey is with a protective figure (often a little old crone or old man) who provides the adventurer with amulets against the dragon forces he is about to pass."[42] In *A New Hope* this is Obi-Wan, who is somewhat replaced in *The Empire Strikes Back* by Yoda. The lightsaber is the amulet, and the dragon is both the Death Star and Darth Vader in *A New Hope*. The dragon also includes Luke's inner temptations as the trilogy continues. Thereafter, the hero must cross the "first threshold," a boundary between safety and the challenges that will make him a hero (best seen in the Cantina), where the hero is joined by partners (Han Solo and Chewbacca), and moves forward into the "belly of the whale" where the hero "is swallowed into the unknown, and would appear to have died" (represented by the Death Star).[43]

As part of this process, and to overcome the great imminent evil, the hero must gain "mystical insight."[44] In an interview with Bill Moyers, Joseph Campbell explained, "What all the myths have to deal with is transformations of consciousness of one kind or another. You have been thinking one way, you now have to think a different way."[45] Obviously, in *Star Wars* this involves the Force, and we hear an echo of Campbell in Yoda, "You must *unlearn* what you have learned" (*The Empire Strikes Back*). This encounter with the supernatural is essential for the success of hero development, and Luke appropriately begins his training in the Force aboard the Millennium Falcon, unknowingly on his way to the Death Star.

Next, the hero encounters the "road of trials," sometimes portrayed as the inescapable trap/maze of the labyrinth, wherein he must meet with the Goddess. Luke's road of trials is in the "belly" of the Death Star, in which he must navigate challenges, rescue the damsel (who at their first encounter stops him in his tracks like a Goddess), and make his escape. Symbolically significant to this stage is the trash compactor scene, which Henderson describes as follows:

> The walls of the room begin to close in on its occupants just before their final release through a small door—rather like the contractions that push a baby out into the world. So on the one hand, the experience is that of being consumed by the Death Star; on the other, this is an ordeal of initiation and rebirth.[46]

The trials have not yet ended, though. To escape the Death Star, our band of would-be-heroes must lose Obi-Wan, the mentor. Henderson explains:

> In the classic structure of the hero's journey, the guide can only bring the hero so far, and Ben has now fulfilled his functions: he has ferried Luke across the preliminary threshold, given him the magic talisman, introduced him to the ways of the Force, found him a pair of hero partners and protectors, brought him to the princess, and enabled him to escape. Luke, as

part of his growth, must let go of his mentor, just as Arthur has to become independent of Merlin once he grows to manhood.[47]

Thereafter, Luke is able to experience his "flight" in escape from the Death Star and return in battle to slay this dragon using his newfound courage, mystical power of the Force, and help from his companions. However, Luke's training as a Jedi and his hero's journey have only begun with *A New Hope*. Consequently, we do not see all of Campbell's stages coming to fruition in this one film. It will take until the end of the original trilogy before Luke continues his "trials" and makes his full "return" from his formation, thereby becoming our hero in the fullest mythical sense. At that point he will become the "master of the two worlds" as Campbell calls it, capable of existing in the realms of the regular world and the Force, as well as becoming a master of his Jedi skills to train a new generation of Jedi.[48] In the process, though, he still must have an experience in the "sacred grove" with Yoda on Dagobah, slay more "dragons," descend into more "underworlds," and achieve "atonement with the father."[49]

Samurai, Westerns, and Nazis

Inspirations for *Star Wars* include several more sources, both ancient and modern. Among the ancient, "Lucas expressed his interest in feudal Japan to artist Ralph McQuarrie when he asked him to come up with the first renderings of the *Star Wars* look and even offered images of samurai warriors for inspiration."[50] Jedi apparel includes a monastic, "medieval European look; and the hooded robe that Ben, Luke, and the Emperor wear is derived from a monk's garb, in order to highlight the Jedi spiritual association," which is strong Catholic imagery.[51] At the same time, the "under robes for the costumes of both Ben and the Emperor [and all Jedi in the prequels] are elegant Japanese kimonos of raw silk."[52] According to Henderson, Lucas's original instruction for Vader to McQuarrie was "a large helmet like that of the Japanese samurai, and a silk mask covering his face," though McQuarrie prevailed in changing the silk mask to a respirator mask in order to fit the space setting of the film.[53] Even the term "Jedi" is "a derivative of the word *Jidaigeki*, the Japanese cinematic term for samurai-filled period dramas set in feudal Nippon."[54] Later *Star Wars* films would include architecture, costumes, and the like from all sorts of cultures. McDowell notes, "Dagobah's naming apparently after an Indian and Burmese Buddhist temple (the Dagoba); and the basing of Qui-Gon Jinn's name on the Chinese meditative and energy manipulating martial-arts discipline *Qi-Gong*."[55] Church teaching says that just as "the Church considers all goodness and truth found in [world] religions as 'a preparation for the Gospel and given by him who enlightens all men that they may at length have life.'"[56] *Star Wars* (an amalgamation of religions and cultures) may serve as a similar "preparation for the Gospel."

Akira Kurosawa's work also had a couple of strong influences upon Lucas. His 1954 Asian film, *Seven Samurai*, impacted Lucas as a film student. Not only did Lucas find Kurosawa's look to be "very exotic," but he also "found it very interesting that nothing was explained. You are thrown into this world… It's like the world of an anthropologist. You walk into this strange society; you sit there and observe it."[57] Lucas employed this in *Star Wars* by avoiding heavy exposition and letting the audience soak it all in. Henderson further explains:

> Lucas particularly admired the look of "immaculate reality" that infused Kurosawa's films. They were meticulously crafted so that nothing looked like a set, nothing looked designed...putting the viewer in the position of an observer just arrived on the scene who needs to catch up with what is going on.[58]

Non-Catholics who are learning about the Catholic Church may relate well to this kind of jarring experience. Catholics would do well to remember what it is like to be thrown into George Lucas's *Star Wars* galaxy without exposition in order to empathetically share the richness of Catholic traditions, rituals, and sacraments with non-Catholics.

Modern source material is also abundant. Lucas incorporated pieces from American Westerns as well because "he saw the Western, which had its golden age in the years following World War II, as a modern mythology that had drifted out of fashion by 1970, and he wanted to recapture some of its glory."[59] Among the elements of the Western are Han Solo as the anti-hero cowboy/gunslinger, Tatooine as the Western frontier, threats from "savages" like the Tusken Raiders, and rough saloon environment of the Mos Eisley cantina.[60] Reflecting on the Western, Lucas says:

> I became very fascinated with how we could replace this mythology that drifted out of

fashion—the Western. One of the prime issues of mythology was that it was always on the frontier, over the hill... And I said, well, the only place we've got left is space—that's the frontier. ... We were just beginning the Space Age, and it was all very alluring to say, gee, we could build a modern mythology out of this mysterious land that we're about to explore.[61]

Consequently, Lucas found himself moving quite naturally into the *Buck Rogers* and *Flash Gordon* science fiction adventures of his youth. We might argue that even beyond the unknown of space is an even greater frontier, that of the spiritual realm, the Kingdom of God, heaven. Just as the Western and space interest audiences, we may also use the allure of the spiritual realm to our advantage.

Parts of the films, especially the Empire and new First Order, are replete with World War II imagery. The trench run on the Death Star at the end of *A New Hope* looks like a World War II bombing run with the precision drop of proton torpedoes into the exhaust port. The Empire and First Order troops are aligned with Nazi symbolism. Consider the speech of Admiral Hux on Starkiller Base before it fires upon the Hosnian System in *The Force Awakens*, for instance. Moreover, the Death Star has been compared to nuclear superweapons and the Imperial Stormtroopers reflect Hitler's SS troopers.[62] Hitler, more specifically, has strong ties to Palpatine. Mary Henderson explains:

> From the leadership of the fledgling Nazi party, [Hitler] got himself appointed chancellor of Germany, then vaulted into the presidency,

which he turned into a dictatorship, declaring himself the "Fuhrer," or supreme leader. Hitler then shut himself away from any real contact with the people; he was surrounded instead by his personal bodyguards, who were pledged to defend him to the death. ... Hitler officially ended the German Republic by passing an act that gave him absolute rule.[63]

These elements closely resemble what we see from Sheev Palpatine as he rises from senator of Naboo to Supreme Chancellor, then manipulates even more power to the point of becoming Emperor of the new Galactic Empire he founded. Finally, he "dissolved the Council permanently" so that "the last remnants of the Old Republic have been swept away," as Grand Moff Tarkin reports in *A New Hope*. From a Catholic perspective, we may juxtapose God's plan and the consequences of sin by considering such evils both in the real world and in *Star Wars*. Subsequently, "Chapter 6: Sith" will include such comparisons.

George's Vision

Summarizing his overall goal, Lucas has stated, "It's the traditional, ritualistic coming-of-age story."[64] Harrison Ford notes, "The themes that George is dealing with are so strong, so primordial: the conflicts between children and their parents. Luke Skywalker was George growing up, George facing conflict and the need to prove himself. And he did, powerfully."[65] "George was somehow able to put the good guys and the bad guys in the mythology in a package that somehow touched us. I don't know how. I guess if you know, everyone would be doing it," sagely comments Frank Oz, the original puppeteer and voice of Yoda.[66]

Lucas clearly used many motifs, myths, and religious concepts from a number of sources to devise a concept of a spiritual power that would appeal to the masses. I believe that any religious group who tries to claim *Star Wars* solely for their faith tradition would be missing Lucas's intention; however, they may certainly draw correlations to better hand on their own tradition to youth. Even Lucas has recognized:

> When the film came out, almost every single religion took *Star Wars* and used it as an example of their religion and were able to relate it to young people and relate the stories specifically to the Bible and to the Koran and the Torah and things… If it's a tool that can be used to make old stories be new and relate to younger people, that's what the whole point was.[67]

Lucas has created a Hollywood phenomenon by appealing to people's innate questions about good and evil, spiritual power, as well as death and the afterlife, while employing a blend of ambiguity and familiarity to make the films universally attractive. Mary Henderson concludes, "*Star Wars* fulfills the basic function of myth: to open our hearts to the dimension of mystery in our lives and to give us some guidance on our own hero's journey."[68] From a Catholic perspective, Steve Skojec reflects:

> George Lucas may or may not have consciously realized what he was saying or the impact it would have, but he touched a nerve in the

consciousness of the 20th century man. I would argue that the resonance of these stories, far from something merely coincidental, is rather a manifestation of a deeper need for a universe where right and wrong are clearly understood, where antiheros [sic] are defeated by actual heros [sic], where faith is a powerful force to be reckoned with, where redemption is possible even at the moment of death, and where in the end, despite everything being stacked against it, good prevails. If that's not Catholic, I don't know what is.[69]

Successfully Navigating an Asteroid Field

Bringing Lucas's vision to the screen would prove to be fraught with peril. In 1973, George Lucas had a rough idea for *Star Wars* that he began to pitch to studios, but it was incomprehensible to people, because it was so different from what was popular. It was Alan Ladd, Jr. of 20th Century Fox who, though he didn't fully understand what Lucas had in mind with *Star Wars*, was willing to take a chance.[70] "I sort of recognized off of *American Graffiti* that he really was a genius, so I just flew with it," Ladd commented.[71] From Lucas's perspective: "[Ladd] understood what talent was, he respected talent, and he was able to say, 'I think this guy is talented, I think we're going to invest in him.' So, Alan Ladd, Jr. invested in me, he did not invest in the movie, and it paid off."[72] Soon thereafter, *American Graffiti* earned 100 million dollars internationally, so Ladd was further justified in taking a chance on Lucas's dream of *Star Wars*.[73]

Using the Force: *Star Wars* and Catholicism

George Lucas was given a budget of 8 million dollars to make the first film, and following the success of *American Graffiti*, Lucas's agent asked 20th Century Fox if he could get more than $200,000 for writing, directing, and producing *Star Wars*.[74] Ladd believed this was reasonable, but Lucas refused more money or "points" from the studio; what he did want were the rights to make the last two films of his *Star Wars* vision.[75] In addition, he asked for a large portion of the merchandising, which had not previously been used as a major source of income for the film industry.[76] As Ladd puts it, "Up until that time, merchandising had been unknown."[77] George Lucas explains:

> When I took over the licensing, I said I'm going to be able to make t-shirts, I'm going to be able to make posters, and I'm going to be able to sell this movie even though the studio won't. So, I managed to get control of pretty much everything that was left over that the studio didn't really care about.[78]

Magnifying the importance of Lucas's contribution to contemporary cinema with merchandising, Gareth Wigan—a former production executive for 20th Century Fox—stated, "George was enormously far-sighted and the studio wasn't, because they didn't know that the world was changing. George did know the world was changing; I mean he changed it."[79]

Once Lucas began preparations for the film, he was forced to build elements from the ground up to realize his vision. In 1975 he founded Industrial Light & Magic (ILM), the first contemporary special effects company for film.[80] The video and special effects by themselves were not enough to captivate an audience and convey the emotional weight Lucas wished to convey, though. With the innovative audio production work of Ben Burtt—including the beeps of R2-D2, lightsabers, blasters, and wookie roars—the other-worldly fantasy scene was greatly enhanced. Finally, adding a musical score from Academy Award winning composer John Williams allowed the film to come to life as a convincing epic adventure. Lucas took a risk with this "old fashioned symphonic score," as he put it, yet it paid off immensely.[81]

Finishing the film was far from a walk in the park in the city of Theed and proved more like escaping a nest of Gundarks. Everything went over budget, over timeline, and 20th Century Fox executives repeatedly demanded that Alan Ladd, Jr. shut down the production of the film before things degraded further.[82] The entire process even put Lucas's health at risk due to stress and fatigue.[83] As Wilkinson says: "When Lucas showed the first rough cut of the movie with no music and some of the special effects missing to a group of fellow directors [and friends], he was faced with embarrassment, giggles and ridicule."[84] Despite daunting odds and challenges from all sides, the film was completed, yet 20th Century Fox couldn't convince theatres to show it.[85] "Even when the trailers were shown in the movie theatres, many people greeted them with laughter and ridicule. Not the most hopeful of beginnings to the biggest series of movies ever."[86]

Dawn of an Empire

On May 25, 1977, *Star Wars* (*A New Hope*, as we now know it) opened across the country in only 37 theatres, yet set 36 house records![87] "One had never seen anything like it. ... It was the first sort of blockbuster," reflects Carrie Fisher.[88] Steven Spielberg comments, "I had never experienced special effects that were so real...I was dazzled. I loved it, because I loved the story and I loved the characters."[89] "Everyone was standing up and applauding. I've never seen anything like this before in my life, and I'll never see it again," remembers Ladd.[90]

In terms of financial success, Lucas explains that most science fiction films of that era made less than 10 million dollars, and great ones made only 16 to 24 million dollars.[91] Gareth Wigan of 20th Century Fox testifies, "The greatest profit that 20th Century Fox had ever made in a single year was 37 million dollars. [In 1977] they made a profit of 79 million dollars. That was *Star Wars.*"[92] Wilkinson explains:

> It is difficult to underestimate the importance of *Star Wars* to the movie industry. Not only did it save Twentieth Century Fox, it arguably halted the box-office slide of the seventies. At the time *Star Wars* was released, Fox's stock was selling at $12 a share. Four years later it was $70 a share.[93]

At the 1978 Academy Awards, *Star Wars* received 11 nominations and won 7. "While it didn't win for best picture, its nomination was quite an achievement for George Lucas and his 'kids' movie,' which earned more money than any movie in history."[94] As an official documentary explains, "George Lucas had helped turn the tide of Hollywood's downbeat realism and brought back a sense of fantasy and wonder. Movies were fun again."[95] David Wilkinson explains, in the 1970s television was reducing people's interest in film, but "*Star Wars* became a defining moment in restoring large audiences to the cinema screens. ... The whole movie industry was revolutionized by *Star Wars*."[96] In addition, Wilkinson notes:

> *Star Wars* introduced the concept of the event movie. There had been a few "blockbusters" before *Star Wars*, most notably *Jaws* in 1975, but movies after *Star Wars* were very different. Merchandising, coupled with a summer release date, raised the profile of blockbuster movies and added to the revenue that cinemas brought in.[97]

Wilkinson further testifies how the franchise effectively launched "the most successful merchandising operations ever and transformed the merchandising concept of movies."[98] He continues, "Up to the launch of *Star Wars*, merchandising had been used to sell movies. After *Star Wars*, movies began to sell the merchandise."[99] The explosion of merchandising and the revenue George Lucas was able to garner from it allowed him to build his own empire and empowered the vision of *Star Wars* to continue nearly *ad infinitum*. Lucas reflects, "This was the perfect opportunity to become independent of the Hollywood system" by financing the production of the sequel on his own, which prevented the studio from meddling with his vision.[100]

The trilogy would conclude with *The Empire Strikes Back* and *Return of the Jedi* together being nominated for 9 Oscars, winning 3 total. The success of the remaining two films would solidify the position of *Star Wars* as cinema legend and position George Lucas as the "sole owner of the most successful franchise in movie history," but Lucas would not stop there.[101] An official documentary explains:

> With the profits he made from the *Star Wars* movies and merchandise, George Lucas was able to keep funding his dream of pushing the boundaries of film and audio technology. For the next two decades he continued to create new and exciting innovations, and in the process he fundamentally changed filmmaking for the better.[102]

As a video producer and editor, one of Lucas's achievements I appreciate most is his contribution to digital video and editing. Wilkinson notes: "In 1984, Lucasfilm revolutionized motion picture editing with Editdroid and Soundroid, the world's first non-linear digital editing systems. For the first time, filmmakers could individually access any video or audio track at the touch of a button."[103] In effect, Lucas helped make the digital editing we do on our home computers possible. "In 1985, Lucasfilm's computer division invented the Pixar computer," later bought out by Disney, which used 3D animation to produce dozens of animated films such as *Toy Story*, *Finding Nemo*, and *Cars*.[104]

After helping to produce the special effects for the 1993 film *Jurassic Park* with ILM, Lucas realized technology was catching up to complement his original vision for *Star Wars*. In 1997, the *Star Wars Trilogy Special Edition* was released, with new scenes and effects added to the original films to make them look the way Lucas had originally intended. Thereafter, he would embark on producing the prequel trilogy with release dates in 1999, 2002, and 2005.

The anticipation for this new trilogy was palpable. When *The Phantom Menace* was released on May 19, 1999, "It is estimated that over 2 million people skipped work on opening day, costing the US economy $300 million in daily production," reports Wilkinson.[105] Following that trilogy, Lucas launched *The Clone Wars* animated theatrical release followed by five seasons of the 3D animated television series before selling Lucasfilm to Disney. *The Clone Wars* won 4 daytime Emmys out of 18 nominations in its last three seasons.

George Lucas's contribution to cinema has been phenomenal, and he launched movie making and marketing onto a new level. Legendary composer, John Williams, testified, "He's created people that everyone in the world knows. Any author that could create such memorable characters would be a very happy person indeed."[106] "His films changed epic productions, he changed storytelling, he created what Hollywood is today," affirms producer Howard Kazanjian.[107] "George Lucas moved us into a new place in space, a new time in the future, which no one had created up to that time. *Star Wars* had a tremendous impact on the young people, as well as adults, for that matter," reflects broadcaster, Walter Kronkite.[108] In his own way, Lucas undertook and completed a heroic adventure.

If people do not directly appreciate the *Star Wars* franchise, they ought to at least appreciate Lucas's contributions to cinema and the impact the franchise has had on our culture. Consider for example, at the time of this writing, fans have compiled a list of *Star*

Wars references in other films totaling nearly 350 (if one only counts *Spaceballs* once), not to mention references in television and other media.[109] *Star Wars* is truly the epic myth of our era.

---

[1] Roy M. Anker, *Catching Light: Looking for God in the Movies* (Grand Rapids, MI: William B. Eerdmans Publishing Company, 2004), 227.

[2] *Star Wars Empire of Dreams: The Story of the Star Wars Trilogy*. DVD. Executive Produced and Directed by Ken Burns. Lucasfilm Ltd., 2004.

[3] David Wilkinson, *The Power of the Force: the Spirituality of the Star Wars Films* (Oxford: Lion, 2000), 62.

[4] Ibid, 62-63.

[5] Ibid, 72.

[6] *Star Wars Empire of Dreams*.

[7] Ibid.

[8] "40 Years of Star Wars Panel," Lucasfilm Ltd. (Star Wars Celebration Orlando, 13 April 2017) https://www.youtube.com/watch?v=YI5QodTtlME (accessed 22 July 2017).

[9] Bill Moyers, *The Mythology of Star Wars with George Lucas and Bill Moyers* (Public Affairs Television, Inc., 1999), https://vimeo.com/groups/183185/videos/38026023 (accessed 21 July 2017).

[10] Dick Staub, *Christian Wisdom of the Jedi Masters* (San Francisco: John Wiley & Sons, 2005), 9.

[11] Mary Henderson, *Star Wars: The Magic of Myth* (New York: Bantam, 1997), 6.

[12] Ibid.

[13] Ibid, 197-198.

[14] Moyers.

[15] "40 Years of Star Wars Panel," Lucasfilm Ltd. (Star Wars Celebration Orlando, 13 April 2017) https://www.youtube.com/watch?v=YI5QodTtlME (accessed 22 July 2017).

[16] Wilkinson, 10.

[17] Ibid.

[18] Ibid, 11.

[19] Steve Skojec, "Star Wars: Catholic Ethos, Universal Appeal," *One Peter Five* (17 December 2015) https://onepeterfive.com/star-wars-catholic-ethos-universal-appeal/ (accessed 24 March 2017).

[20] Ibid.

[21] Moyers.

[22] *Star Wars Empire of Dreams.*
[23] Skojec.
[24] *Star Wars Empire of Dreams.*
[25] Ibid.
[26] Ibid.
[27] Ibid.
[28] Ibid.
[29] Moyers.
[30] Ibid.
[31] Anker, 242.
[32] Moyers.
[33] Ibid.
[34] Anker, 241.
[35] Henderson, 19; Joseph Campbell, *The Hero with a Thousand Faces*, 3rd ed. (Novato, CA: New World Library, 2008), 41.
[36] Wilkinson, 100.
[37] Henderson, 20.
[38] Ibid.
[39] James L. Papandrea, *From Star Wars to Superman: Christ Figures in Science Fiction and Superhero Films* (Manchester, NH: Sophia Institute Press, 2017), 72.
[40] Anker, 225.
[41] Henderson, 29.
[42] Campbell, 57.
[43] Ibid, 64-74.
[44] Henderson, 44.
[45] Ibid.
[46] Ibid, 54.
[47] Ibid, 57.
[48] Campbell, 196.
[49] Henderson, 68, 106, & 107.
[50] Ibid, 186.
[51] Ibid.
[52] Ibid.
[53] Ibid, 189.
[54] Skojec.

55 John C. McDowell, *The Gospel According to Star Wars: Faith, Hope, and the Force* (Louisville, Westminster John Knox Press, 2007), 21.

56 *Catechism of the Catholic Church*, 2d ed. (Citta del Vaticano: Libreria Editrice Vaticana, 1997), § 843.

57 Henderson, 133.

58 Ibid.

59 Ibid, 126.

60 Ibid, 129.

61 Ibid, 136.

62 Ibid, 145-146.

63 Ibid, 146.

64 *Star Wars Empire of Dreams*.

65 Ibid.

66 Ibid.

67 Moyers.

68 Henderson, 198.

69 Skojec.

70 *Star Wars Empire of Dreams*.

71 Ibid.

72 Ibid.

73 Ibid.

74 Ibid.

75 Ibid.

76 Ibid.

77 Ibid.

78 Ibid.

79 Ibid.

80 Ibid.

81 Ibid.

82 Ibid.

83 Ibid.

84 Wilkinson, 20; *Star Wars Empire of Dreams*.

85 *Star Wars Empire of Dreams*.

86 Wilkinson, 20.

87 *Star Wars Empire of Dreams*.

88 Ibid.

89 Ibid.

[90] Ibid.
[91] Ibid.
[92] Ibid.
[93] Wilkinson, 32.
[94] *Star Wars Empire of Dreams*.
[95] Ibid.
[96] Wilkinson, 32.
[97] Ibid, 33.
[98] Ibid, 51-52.
[99] Ibid.
[100] *Star Wars Empire of Dreams*.
[101] Ibid.
[102] Ibid.
[103] Ibid.
[104] Ibid.
[105] Wilkinson, 44.
[106] *Star Wars Empire of Dreams*.
[107] Ibid.
[108] Ibid.//
[109] "List of References to *Star Wars* in Movies," *Star Wars Fanpedia*, http://starwarsfans.wikia.com/wiki/List_of_references_to_Star_Wars_in_movies (accessed 22 July 2017).

Chapter 3: What the Force is Not

"That's not how the Force works!"
– Han Solo (*The Force Awakens*)

When approaching a great, transcendent mystery—something we humans can understand only in a limited way—it is often helpful to employ negative theology. In other words, to understand a rich spiritual concept, a fruitful place to start is through a process of elimination by which we identify what is not true. For the early Christians, grasping the concepts of the Trinity and the Incarnation of Jesus as fully God and fully man are great examples. To arrive at an understanding of the Trinity, the Councils of Nicaea and Constantinople in the Fourth Century took a critical look at each of the three persons—what they shared and what made them distinct—from a process of elimination to a consensus of affirmation. Thereafter in the Fifth Century when considering the personhood of Jesus, the Councils of Ephesus and Chalcedon came to a positive consensus about Christ after ruling out numerous errors. Similarly, to approach the topic of the Force, the spiritual aspect of the *Star Wars* universe, we may begin by exploring what the Force is not (negative theology) before moving on to determine what the force is (positive theology) in the following chapter.

Dualism

In 1983, George Lucas told *Time* magazine that the Force was God, but "sixteen years later, Lucas told Bill Moyers that he put the Force into Star Wars 'to try to awaken a certain kind of spirituality in young people—more a belief in God than a belief in any particular religious system.'"[1] Some critics see a conflict with Christianity: "If the Force is the supreme power in the Star Wars universe, its ability to embody good and evil differentiates it from many religions, including Christianity, Judaism and Islam, which preach that God personifies only good."[2] This causes a problem for Christians who want to see the Force as representing God, because it presents a dualistic theology. Dualism sees good and evil in *equal* opposition. It explains that evil exists in the world, because God is not omnipotent, and thus there is another equal power working in opposition to God. Conversely, Christianity recognizes the good and evil in the world, but good rules supreme. God, who is all good, is also the creator of everything, and he only creates what is good. Thus, all evil is merely a corruption of the original good.

Using the Force: *Star Wars* and Catholicism

Admittedly, at first glance the Force seems dualistic with a good side and bad, equally locked in opposition. In fact, Lucas himself has made statements that are quite dualistic regarding his intention behind the Force as two sides of the same essence. However, information from the films seems to suggest this is not the case, so much so that McDowell comments, "What I am suggesting is that Lucas's practice (his movies) is theologically much better than his theory (his theological understandings)."[3] Even though Lucas may have initially intended to create a dualistic Force, it did not materialize as such. A deeper exploration of this issue is in order, as this is an important topic for the relationship between *Star Wars* and Catholicism.

When Anakin is seduced by the dark side of the Force in *Episode III: Revenge of the Sith*, his former teacher, Obi-Wan Kenobi, says to him, "You were the Chosen One! It was said that you would destroy the Sith, not join them. It was you who would bring balance to the Force, not leave it in Darkness." Anker explains, "Obi-Wan is after nothing less than the defeat of Darkness itself, the metaphysical power that seeks to destroy all that is good in the world."[4] "Balance" here is the eradication of evil and the maintaining of good, not good and evil balancing out. An official *Star Wars* source explains what Qui-Gon Jinn believed about the prophecy Obi-Wan references: "Anakin is the 'Chosen One' of an ancient prophecy, and is destined to become a Jedi, destroy the Sith, and bring balance to the Force."[5] If it is true that the Force is dualistic, how could destroying those who practice the dark side bring it back into "balance," or how would it be prophetically possible to eliminate evil? For Dualism to hold, "balance" would have to be an eternal struggle between light and dark. Instead, this *Star Wars* prophecy parallels Christian eschatology of the second coming of Christ described in Revelation where evil will be defeated and good will reign.

Supervising director of *The Clone Wars*, Dave Filoni, was commenting at a panel about why he likes the change from the old Anakin Force ghost to the young Anakin Force ghost in the Special Edition version of *Return of the Jedi*:

> It doesn't make sense, mythologically, for him to maintain the guise of the old man afterward in the Force, because he was never good. He was never balanced when he was that person. He was the wicked old man, so he has to shed that skin like everything else. So he appears as a young man.[6]

Here Filoni equates Anakin being "balanced" with him being good. Filoni worked at the right hand of George Lucas for almost a decade on *The Clone Wars* series and learned the deepest secrets of the Force from him, so his understanding of what being balanced means to the Jedi is significant.

In *Revenge of the Sith*, Darth Sidious, an evil Sith Lord, tempts Anakin saying, "If one is to understand the great mystery [the Force], one must study all its aspects, not just the dogmatic, narrow view of the Jedi. If you wish to become a complete and wise leader, you must embrace a larger view of the Force" (*Revenge of the Sith*). If one attempts to "balance" both sides in Sidious's dualistic fashion, opening his or her mind to the "greater mystery of the Force" in such a way, this seems to result in becoming totally dark, as Darth

Sidious's character demonstrates. A Christian cannot "open-mindedly" cultivate both sin and virtue in his or her life and expect those mutually exclusive dispositions to be compatible. That is not a viable "balance" but rather a giving in to the corruption of evil, which is exactly what Sidious is attempting by tempting Anakin.

I suggest, based on evidence from *Star Wars* lore, that the true nature of the Force is good, only good, and maintains "balance" only in the absence of evil. The dark side is thus a perverted version of the true Force. Obi-Wan, for example, implies that the Force's true nature is good, and it is out of balance only because the Sith have perverted it for evil. McDowell observes:

> The characters use the language of the Force without qualification when speaking specifically of the good, whereas evil has to be specified. The force *is* the Good itself and that is why they do not speak of the good side of the Force.[7]

Lucas has even referred to the dark side as, "like a huge cancer, alive, festering."[8] Cancer may be genetically related to the original organism, but it is a perversion of the DNA to the point of threatening the life of the entire organism.

We find additional evidence in the *Ahsoka* novel. While Ahsoka's use of the Force is natural and harmonious, the book clearly indicates the "unnaturalness" of how a dark side inquisitor uses the Force.[9] Moreover, the reason dark side lightsabers are red is that they "bleed," becoming red rather than their original color when "corrupted" by the dark side.[10] [SPOILERS in the remainder of the paragraph.] In the

Ahsoka novel, Ahsoka took two red kyber crystals from the lightsaber of an inquisitor she killed in combat in order to construct two new lightsabers for herself. Once she took possession of them, they changed from red to white. Ahsoka says she "freed" and "restored" the kybers.[11] It is as if the Force flows naturally with the good but is twisted or compelled by the dark, and this is even evident in the "living" kyber crystals.

Instead of the Force being Dualistic, the idea more closely correlates to Catholicism's understanding of good and evil. Catholicism sees all God created as good. There were those angels, however, who turned against the natural order of things, rebelled against God, and became demons. Satan and the fallen angels constitute the evil spiritual force present in the world, but they are not equal in power to God. The *Catechism of the Catholic Church* explains, "This 'fall' consists in the free choice of these created spirits, who radically and irrevocably rejected God and his reign."[12] Evil is then a corruption and distortion of the truth and the good.

If the Force is not dualistic, as we have seen, then the light side must be stronger. When young Luke Skywalker asks the great Jedi Master, Yoda, "Is the dark side stronger?" in *Episode V: The Empire Strikes Back*, Yoda's reply is a thrice, "No...no...no. Quicker, easier, more seductive." Surely, the dark side is not stronger. However, Yoda does not outright affirm that the light is stronger. One point we may consider to make such a case is that Jedi achieve a higher power than the Sith.

While the Sith selfishly crave absolute power and immortality, the selfless Jedi are the only ones allowed to achieve immortality through the Force, and their power is in union with the Force rather than extracted from it. That union allows them to be built up in relationship with the Force, while the Sith tension with the dark side only disfigures them further, making them progressively less human. Sith become plagiarized corruptions of their originally good selves, much like a human mired in sin.

The weakness of this assertion is that there are more Force wielders than the Jedi and Sith, such as the Ones from Mortis, Force Priestesses from the Force planet, the Bendu on Atollon, the Nightsisters of Dathomir, and Force users of no allegiance like adult Ahsoka Tano. We know too little about all Force users, let alone the Force itself, to come to a conclusion about whether the light is definitively stronger than the dark, but we can make a strong case for it with the previous information about what "balance" in the Force means.

Nevertheless, when we look at the additional Force users portrayed in *Star Wars* canon, the evidence continues to support a Christian interpretation. For example, those who claim neutrality in the Force are not half good and a half evil—they are essentially good. Adult Ahsoka is one obvious example. Even though she is no Jedi, she is balanced in the light. Another is the Bendu, an ancient Force-sensitive being who mentors Kanan Jarrus in *Rebels* season 3. The Bendu says of himself, "I'm the one in the middle," meaning between light and dark with no allegiance to either side, yet he is definitively not evil, he is more indifferent in his promotion of either side.

Even among the Ones on Mortis in season 3 of *The Clone Wars* [SPOILERS], while Daughter is the embodiment of the light as the Son is of the dark, the Father, who is supposed to maintain the balance between them, is actually quite benevolent. True, he may be indifferent and callus at times, like the Bendu, but he's essentially good. The Father on Mortis even tells the Son he "held hope that [the Son] could resist the dark side," and that he loves his son. His last words to his son are, "I always knew there was good in you." These are not the words of a purely neutral Force wielder "balancing" light and dark at 50% each. Rather, they are "balanced" in the light only—what I have defended as the true nature of the Force. What they refer to as being in the "middle" is that they have no allegiance to the Jedi or the Sith, what seems to be an indifference to the sides, but it is clear that they are essentially benevolent, which supports the idea that the Force is essentially good as well. Perhaps they are indifferent to the two sides of the Force, because they are simply in tune with the Force itself, which I have defended as the light side only. They may find the dark side not worth mentioning or even recognizing, because it is a mere perversion of the Force.

Pantheism

Yoda presents other potentially conflicting views regarding Christianity and the Force. He expounds on the Force in *The Empire Strikes Back* when he instructs:

> My ally is the Force. And a powerful ally it is. Life creates it, makes it grow. Its energy surrounds us and binds us. Luminous beings are we, not this crude matter. You must feel the Force around you. Here, between you, me, the tree, the rock, everywhere!

He seems to suggest that the Force may be pantheistic— the idea that God and the universe are the same, and

God is in everything—thus tying God to creation. Christianity sees God as separate from and beyond his creation, yet present all throughout it.

The Force is a creation itself, from all living beings, so it does coincide with pantheism if one sees it as being God. However, I caution the direct correlation between the Force and the Christian God, not only because it may lead to this conclusion, but also because the correlation is weak, and even Lucas retreated from this idea. When asked, "Is the Force God?," George Lucas replied:

> I put the Force in the movies in order to try to awaken a certain kind of spirituality in young people, more a belief in God than a belief in any particular, you know, religious system. I mean the real question is to ask the question, because if you haven't enough interest in the mysteries of life to ask the questions, is there a God or is there not a God, that's for me the worst thing that can happen. ... I think you should have an opinion about that. ... I think there is a God, no question, what that God is or what we know about that God I'm not sure.[13]

Lucas's uncertainty about the nature or inherent truths of God contributes to the ambiguity found throughout *Star Wars*. Nevertheless, his Christian background seems to have prevailed in his thought enough to allow *Star Wars* to be predominantly Christian, as we will continue to explore, especially in the next chapter.

Gnosticism

Yoda's statement, "Luminous beings are we, not this crude matter," requires additional discussion. This may seem to relate to another ideology known as Gnosticism—which is Dualistic in nature—where the physical world is seen as evil and the spirit world is good. Catholicism denounces this position, because we see all of creation as inherently good; "God looked at everything he had made, and he found it very good" (Gn 1:31). Furthermore, Jesus took on physical form, and we receive him physically in the Eucharist. Physical and material does not equate to evil for a Catholic. In fact, especially as the sacraments and incarnation indicate, God uses them for very holy and sacred purposes.

I believe Yoda is explaining to a young Luke that there is something beyond the physical realm, but he does not take it so far as to say the physical is bad. Luke lives in a universe where people rarely speak of something beyond the physical. The idea of a spiritual realm is largely beyond his comprehension at this point, and it is not common in popular thought throughout the *Star Wars* galaxy during the later reign of the Empire. Yoda is explaining that what we are goes beyond our "crude matter" bodies. We are also spiritual, but not to the exclusion of the physical. Here Yoda overemphasizes the spiritual to make a point. In fact, even a Jedi uses the Force to act in the physical; they train their bodies in physical skills which heighten their knowledge of the Force. In addition, the Force is present in and created by all living things, so Yoda cannot be referring to "crude matter" as bad. Thus, the Jedi are clearly not Gnostics.

Person or Power

There are other major problems to address between Christian thought and the Force. Greene states, "God is central to Christian and Jewish belief systems, being a personal deity who interacts with the world, not an energy field as is the Force".[14] Greene here, and many others as well, misses that the Force does have some personal attributes, most notably a will. In *Episode I: The Phantom Menace*, Jedi Knight Qui-Gon Jinn says, "Finding [Anakin] was the will of the Force...I have no doubt of that," and, "Our meeting was not a coincidence. Nothing happens by accident." Though the Force is an energy field, it has a will, and it interacts with the world to make that will a reality. Profoundly, Darth Sidious recalls, "Darth Plagueis had once remarked that, 'The Force can strike back,' ... and indeed Sidious could see evidence of that sometimes even in Vader. The barest flicker of persistent light."[15] Sidious's goal was to make sure "whatever faint light of hope remained could be snuffed out for good" so that the "Force could not strike back."[16] Not only does this statement reinforce the earlier assertion that evil is merely corrupted goodness, it also confirms that the Force has a will. It further appears that the Force will not allow a total corruption of the light. Having a will gives it a personal quality, not being merely an impersonal, spiritual power like the Tao of Chinese folk religion.

---

[1] Mark I. Pinsky, "Battle of All Faiths Builds Over Lessons of Star Wars Films," *Edmonton Journal* (Alberta), 4 June 2005, B13.

[2] Amanda Greene, "Faith & the Force," *Star News* (Wilmington, NC), 21 May 2005, 1D, 4D.

[3] John C. McDowell, *The Gospel According to Star Wars: Faith, Hope, and the Force* (Louisville, Westminster John Knox Press, 2007), 42.

[4] Roy M. Anker, *Catching Light: Looking for God in the Movies* (Grand Rapids, MI: William B. Eerdmans Publishing Company, 2004), 222.

[5] *Ultimate Star Wars* (New York: DK Penguin Random House, 2015), 22.

[6] "Force Ghosts – The Lost Missions Q&A, Star Wars: The Clone Wars," Star Wars Youtube Channel (published 4 December 2014) https://www.youtube.com/watch?v=iKWDZaxUoMg (accessed 26 July 2017).

[7] McDowell, 28.

[8] Ibid.

[9] E. K. Johnston, *Star Wars: Ahsoka*, Audiobook narrated by Ashley Eckstein (Random House Audio, 2016), approximately 5:18:00.

[10] Ibid., approximately 5:52:00.

[11] Ibid., approximately 6:53:00.

[12] *Catechism of the Catholic Church*, 2d ed. (Citta del Vaticano: Libreria Editrice Vaticana, 1997), § 392.

[13] Bill Moyers, *The Mythology of Star Wars with George Lucas and Bill Moyers* (Public Affairs Television, Inc., 1999), https://vimeo.com/groups/183185/videos/38026023 (accessed 21 July 2017).

[14] Greene.

[15] James Luceno, *Star Wars: Tarkin*, Audiobook narrated by Euan Morton (Random House Audio, 2014), approximately 3:44:00.

[16] Ibid.

Chapter 4: The Nature of the Force

"You must feel the Force around you."
– Yoda (*The Empire Strikes Back*)

For those well versed in *Star Wars*, no explanation of the Force is necessary, though I will offer a synopsis from the franchise before progressing into a theological reflection on the Force. Ultimately, the Force is a mystery beyond comprehension and represents the spiritual power in the *Star Wars* universe. The most basic explanations come from Obi-Wan and Yoda in *A New Hope* and *The Empire Strikes Back*, respectively.

Our first exposure to this concept is in Obi-Wan's home on Tatooine in *A New Hope*: "The Force is what gives a Jedi his power. It's an energy field created by all living things. It surrounds us and penetrates us. It binds the galaxy together." Roy M. Anker sees this as relating to Ephesians 4:6, "One God and Father of all, who is over all and through all and in all."[1] In *The Empire Strikes Back*, Yoda describes the Force as his "powerful ally" and continues: "Life creates it, makes it grow. Its energy surrounds us and binds us. Luminous beings are we, not this crude matter. You must feel the Force around you. Here, between you, me, the tree, the rock, everywhere!"

According to the official *Star Wars* Databank, there are two parts to the Force, the living Force and the cosmic Force. The living Force is present in all life forms, and the cosmic Force is the "timeless" spiritual entity/power that exists beyond matter.[2] The living Force seems more pantheistic while the cosmic force is the component more closely resembling Christian belief.

In *The Clone Wars*, Yoda visits a Force Planet in order to learn the path to immortality from Force Priestesses. This planet "is a mystical world and the foundation of life itself. It is the birthplace of the midichlorians, microscopic organisms that connect the living Force to the cosmic Force."[3] Explaining the planet and the relationship of the living and cosmic Force, Yoda's priestess guide states, "When a living thing dies, all is renewed. Life passes from the living Force into the cosmic Force and becomes one with it. One powers the other. One is renewed by the other." This appears to be another example how Lucas's vision amalgamates differing, even conflicting, spiritual views into *Star Wars*.

Using the Force: *Star Wars* and Catholicism

Each of the *Star Wars* films seems to build upon each other to reveal more about the Force. It is similar to the way God gradually revealed himself to the Hebrew people and echoes Christ's words, "I have much more to tell you, but you cannot bear it now" (Jn 16:12). Similarly, Lucas gives us fragments to digest regarding this "one all-powerful Force controlling everything," as Han Solo states in *A New Hope*. Perhaps the Force is how the Jedi conceive of everything even remotely spiritual, hence the broad use of the term. If we were to lump the triune God, saints, angels, demons, Satan, and all supernatural events into one, perhaps that is similar to how the Jedi view the Force. Lucas made the Force intentionally vague to appeal to multiple cultures and religious ideologies, and it may be perfectly plausible to apply different Christian elements to the Force at different times.

Reverence

Even throughout the *Star Wars* franchise, the Force is treated in different ways at different periods in time. Marc Barnes explains:

> In the originals, access to the Force occurred on the basis of faith and asceticism. Luke Skywalker had to cease trusting his physical eyes and take on the eyes of faith; he had to train his body and mind extensively before he was capable of the same feats of the Force as Yoda.[4]

The prequels, however, "departed from this religious heart, by making the Force something embedded in the natural world," by linking it to one's midi-chlorian count.⁵ Barnes continues, "The Jedi of the originals were concerned with *not* using the Force… But in the prequels, the Force loses its sacred status and becomes a magic weapon," and therefore a sense of reverence is lost.⁶

There are many elements from the prequels not well received by long-time fans of the franchise, and the midi-chlorians are among them. Since midi-chlorians are scarcely mentioned outside *The Phantom Menace*, some fans choose to ignore them entirely. Lucas wished to include them to introduce a theme of symbiotic relationship with nature.⁷

Barnes has a point about the Force of *The Phantom Menace* becoming embedded in the physical world. However, I suggest that midi-chlorians may not pose such a large problem since they reside in "all living cells," according to Qui-Gon. They are not the Force itself; and they speak to their host, revealing the "will of the Force." True, those with a high count may be able to sense and use the Force more powerfully than the masses, but there are also those of us in reality who have stronger spiritual senses and more fantastic spiritual gifts. We all have access to God just as all living cells have midi-chlorians and are thus connected to the Force. Counterintuitively, people with less natural ability often achieve more than the naturally gifted both in *Star Wars* and reality, especially by the will of the Force or God, respectively.

Since those who use the Force are so rare after the prequel trilogy in *Star Wars* chronology, it takes on a more transcendent existence, and our attitude toward it is more reverent. In *The Force Awakens,* Barnes notes, "Han Solo derides Finn's blithe mechanization of the Force as an easy answer to the problem of how to disable some shields: 'That's not how the Force works!'"[8] In *Rogue One* we witness Chirrut Îmwe "who trusts the Force, not as a power to be manipulated, but as an object of prayer."[9] The mantra he repeats during his Force walk is "I'm one with the Force, and the Force is with me." The difference here is striking as Barnes notices, "Îmwe 'prays' as he walks through the field of lasers, but we don't see bolts careening off by the swipe of an unseen hand. It is Îmwe who must change in accordance with the Force. It guides him, not vice versa."[10] For those of us looking at the franchise through a Catholic lens, this is a welcome scene, as it correlates with reality. We must conform to God's will, not vice versa.

Admittedly, *Star Wars* fails to be internally consistent in all things, so this may be just another example of that weakness, though it seems reasonable attitudes toward the Force will naturally change with different eras, as we see in reality with people's attitudes toward spirituality and God. The attitude of the prequels may also have contributed to the downfall of the Jedi, perhaps due to their lack of reverence. With wisdom Barnes concludes:

> We do not hear the iconic line, "Use the Force," in *Rogue One*. We hear a reverent one: "Trust the Force." ... Magic wishes to use supernatural powers for material ends. Religion wishes to subordinate material ends to a good and wise supernatural power. *Rogue One* elevates the disciple over the magician and the saint over the technician.[11]

Perhaps if the Jedi at the end of the Old Republic were more like Chirrut Îmwe, they could have sensed the evil plot at work and avoided their demise.

Love

Since the Force does not correlate well to God himself, it may be better compared to an aspect, or many aspects, of God. Anker offers a profound possibility about the essence of the Force by proposing that the Force is love itself.[12] God is love, but love does not entirely encompass God. It is an attribute, but not the entirety. Perhaps the Force is an element of the divine which exists for eternity as one of his characteristics, and it has supernatural, spiritual power. If the Force were a characteristic of God, it is no wonder there is such confusion over what the Force is. The concept of God is intensely deep and difficult to understand, even in the wake of divine revelation. Christianity has spent two millennia unpacking the deposit of faith and revelation received through Christ, much like the Jedi spent millennia trying to understand the Force. Anker explains:

> The Force is an ever-present supernatural reality whose inmost character is a love that bids all to heed and embrace its redemptive call. Its sacred purpose is to bring everything—the whole of creation, in fact, to reconciliation, and thus to harmony and felicity.[13]

Anker taps into the reason why the *Star Wars* films have become such a phenomenon uniting religion and popular culture as well as igniting so much interest from such a diversity of religious groups. Barnes testifies:

> The Force is far more than another weapon for the macho superhero to add to his blaster-belt; rather, it has a very demanding spiritual and moral content. Believing in the Force is easy enough, especially after witnessing its power, as Luke already has; it is quite another matter to understand and embrace—in short, to live—its deepest intentions. ... What it is really about is radical love for all things, a posture its devotees must take deeply into themselves if they wish to become full-fledged Jedis. Beyond all the blasters and monsters and space heroes, the genius and ultimately the lasting appeal of the *Star Wars* saga lies in Lucas's ability to dramatize the necessity, cogency, and poignance of this sacred existential posture in both the lives of his characters and the history of their fictional galaxy. Ultimately, the history of the universe depends not on Luke Skywalker's physical brawn, combat prowess, or strategic wiliness but on the extent to which he has imbibed the lessons of love.[14]

This principle is one that unites religions around the world and is recognized as a staple of human relation and interaction, though it has special connections to Christianity. With the Force, Lucas touches on one of the deepest realities of religion, humanity, and culture.

The Christian, like the Jedi, understands the implications of a radical love, as exemplified by Christ. It requires an intense renunciation of evil, a selfless love for all, and personal sacrifice combined with conversion. When he realizes that he finally has become a Jedi, Luke embodies the renunciation of evil. At the end of *Return of the Jedi*, Luke proclaims, "Never! I'll never turn to the dark side. You've failed, Your Highness. I am a Jedi, like my father before me." Luke renounces the dark side, which is selfishness and hate, the opposites of love. Jesus teaches that the greatest commandment is to love, to love God and to love each other (Mt 22:37-39), even our enemies (Mt 5:44). When Luke learned this, he became a Jedi.

Anakin explained the difference between the Jedi and the Sith in *Revenge of the Sith*, "The Sith rely on their passion for their strength. They think inward, only about themselves. ... The Jedi are selfless...they only care about others." Love turned inward distorts and corrupts, while love directed out is powerful, redemptive, and fulfills its true nature. Luke practiced this love selflessly and with sacrifice when he was willing to die rather than kill Darth Vader, his father. In this action, Vader's heart was turned back to love, for love begets love. As a result, Vader converted; destroyed his master, Darth Sidious (who represents Satan and evil overall); and made his self-sacrificial offering. Anakin died destroying the incarnation of evil and hate, thus redeeming himself, fulfilling the prophecy, and bringing balance back to the Force. The Jedi, strong in the Force, exemplify what a good Christian, strong in the Spirit and love, should be.

The idea of the Force as love works wonderfully with what the Jedi have to teach about its nature. Recall Obi-Wan's teaching in *A New Hope*; "The Force is what gives a Jedi his power. It's an energy field created by all living things. It surrounds us and penetrates us. It binds the galaxy together." Love is what gives a Christian his power, it is a grace of God, who is love. Love surrounds us, penetrates us, and binds all of creation together. Without it, all of creation would be lost. Since love is an attribute of God, the Force as love may be related to God, though not exactly being God, thereby avoiding pitfalls like pantheism.

Holy Spirit

The Force also has similarities to the Holy Spirit. Though the Spirit is not an energy field created by all living things, it does give people power in the form of gifts. In addition, it is omnipresent and may even be seen as binding all of creation together. This seems to be the preferred perspective of Joshua Hays: "The biblical alternative to the Force is the Third Person of the Trinity, the Holy Spirit."[15] He continues:

> Far too many Christians operate virtually unaware of the Spirit's presence and power, just as Luke Skywalker spent his adolescence utterly ignorant of the Force. Perhaps the Spirit is so elusive precisely because it is so ubiquitous. Like the Force, it surrounds us, penetrates us, and binds us together with one another. Many Christians all too easily overlook the Spirit because they encounter it so often and so immediately. They neglect the Spirit in much the same way that a fish might neglect water.[16]

There are also differences, though. The Spirit is a person, rather than a cosmic force, and it cannot be commanded as the Force may be, yet it may be called upon.

Mortis

Like many details from *Star Wars*, we discover more about the Force in *The Clone Wars*. [SPOILERS in this whole "Mortis" section.] We receive ample fodder for thought in the three episodes of the Mortis arc during Season 3 where a few visions occur, such as Qui-Gon visiting both Obi-Wan and Anakin, as well as an older Ahsoka visiting her younger self. Doubt persists, however, because the entire three episode arc is in the context of Anakin, Obi-Wan, and Ahsoka being unconscious on their ship, calling into question the reliability of the entire Mortis experience. For those unaware, Mortis is a planet explained to be a conduit through which all of the Force flows through the galaxy, and "some believe Mortis may be the very origin of the Force itself."[17] In one of the episodes, Obi-Wan tells Anakin, "The planet is the Force."

On Mortis they encounter three beings known as "The Ones" who are identified as "Force wielders."[18] This trio is a family (echoing the Trinity to a degree) with the Father, the Son, and the Daughter.[19] The two children are "the embodiments of selflessness and selfishness," as Daughter is oriented with the light side of the Force, while Son is aligned with the dark.[20] The Father is the only one who is able to "maintain balance" between his children—whom he keeps bound to the realm of Mortis. The Father restrains them on Mortis mostly to prevent his Son from fulfilling his desire to "wreak havoc in the galaxy." The Father seems to have summoned Anakin to Mortis in order to test whether he is the Chosen One of prophecy.[21]

The episodes give us a fascinating glimpse into the Force and numerous prophecies and visions of the future, including a vision Anakin has of himself becoming Darth Vader—one that the Father erases from his memory before he leaves. We also see heroic acts of selflessness. During their stay on Mortis, the Son kills Ahsoka. After the Son also kills the Daughter, the Daughter selflessly offers her life-force to bring Ahsoka back to life, which is achieved through the combined power of Anakin and the Father. At the end of the episodes, the Father dies, and his last words to Anakin are, "You are the Chosen One. You have brought balance to this world, stay on this path and you will do it again for the galaxy, but *beware your heart.*" Interestingly, bringing balance to Mortis is achieved by killing the Son, who slew Daughter, and which led to the death of Father as well. This is a further prophecy of Anakin's significance, his weakness, and the sacrifice and death to occur at the end of Anakin's life.

Mystery

When one begins to look carefully at *Star Wars* with a Christian lens, the connections are bountiful. In the end, though, we must admit that we cannot know everything about the Force, as we cannot know everything about God. Many different ideas may work for the Force in different instances. What we must realize is that the concept of the Force is a bit dynamic and not totally understood. These ideas are so intertwined that it is often difficult to differentiate exactly what the Force relates to best. I propose that just as the triune God is a Christian mystery, so too the Force is a *Star Wars* mystery. We cannot fully grasp the Force in its entirety, but we can apply comparisons to it—like God, Spirit, and love—to better understand it.

---

[1] Roy M. Anker, *Catching Light: Looking for God in the Movies* (Grand Rapids, MI: William B. Eerdmans Publishing Company, 2004), 224.

[2] "Force Priestesses," *Star Wars Databank*, http://www.starwars.com/databank/force-priestesses (accessed 27 July 2017).

[3] "Force Planet," *Star Wars Databank*, http://www.starwars.com/databank/force-planet (accessed 27 July 2017).

[4] Marc Barnes, "Rogue One and the Return of Reverence," *First Things* (3 January 2017) https://www.firstthings.com/web-exclusives/2017/01/rogue-one-and-the-return-of-reverence (accessed 24 March 2017).

[5] Ibid.

[6] Ibid.

[7] Bill Moyers, *The Mythology of Star Wars with George Lucas and Bill Moyers* (Public Affairs Television, Inc., 1999), https://vimeo.com/groups/183185/videos/38026023 (accessed 21 July 2017).

[8] Marc Barnes, "Rogue One and the Return of Reverence," *First Things* (3 January 2017) https://www.firstthings.com/web-exclusives/2017/01/rogue-one-and-the-return-of-reverence (accessed 24 March 2017).

[9] Ibid.

[10] Ibid.

[11] Ibid.

[12] Anker, 237.

[13] Ibid., 241.

[14] Ibid., 228-229.

[15] Joshua Hays, *A True Hope: Jedi Perils and the Way of Jesus* (Macon, GA: Smyth & Helwys, 2015), 62.

[16] Ibid.

[17] *Ultimate Star Wars* (New York: DK Penguin Random House, 2015), 194.

[18] Ibid., 100.

[19] Ibid.

[20] Ibid., 100 & 196.

[21] Ibid., 100.

Chapter 5: Jedi

"I am a Jedi, like my father before me."
– Luke Skywalker (*Return of the Jedi*)

The Jedi are the principal light side Force users of the galaxy. They also bear many similarities to Catholicism and offer lessons valuable for us to consider. This chapter will explore several links between the Jedi and Catholicism.

Jedi Charisms

Jedi seem to have individual and distinct gifts to use the Force in different ways. In the *Ahsoka* novel, Ahsoka explains that force-sensitive younglings have a natural ability to use the Force in a particular way. Only when trained by the Jedi do younglings become able to develop other gifts of the Force. It is this usually singular, exceptional ability that identifies them as Force users and prompted the Jedi to bring them into their formation program. During the Old Republic most

Jedi were "identified within six months of [their] birth and [began] Jedi training immediately so that [they] can learn to control emotions of fear and anger at an early age."[1]

A few are found later, like Ahsoka who was discovered by Master Plo Koon on Shili when she was three years old, though we do not know what Force abilities, like charisms, she manifested.[2] Anakin was much older, and it was his ability to see a short distance into the future, which made him appear to have such quick reflexes, that revealed his Force-sensitivity. After the fall of the Republic and the slaughter of the Jedi, Ahsoka finds herself on the planet Thabesca where she meets a Force-sensitive young girl named Hedala Fardi whose gift was sensitivity to other Force-sensitive beings.[3] When Hedala was being tracked by a dark side inquisitor, she sensed a "shadow" and hid from its search by not using the Force in any way. In *Rebels*, "Kanan Jarrus recognizes Ezra Bridger's keen abilities to sense things before they happen and perform extraordinary physical feats," in order to tip him off to Ezra's Force sensitivity.[4] Thereafter, Kanan offers to train Ezra. About one year after Luke destroyed the first Death Star, he lacks a mentor, and struggles to learn about the Force. Discussing his basic abilities or charisms with a love interest, Luke notes:

> Right now I can kind of feel the Force… It gives me heightened reflexes in battles and maybe a tiny bit of predictive ability, like I'm really good at guessing how the other guy is going to move next. But I'm sure that's just the first step into a larger world.[5]

Using the Force: *Star Wars* and Catholicism

Luke's initial gift is likely similar to his father's.

Sometimes a Jedi may have an incredibly unique gift, such as Quinlan Vos who had the Force gift of "psychometry," which gave him the "ability to perceive the memories of others by touching objects that they handled."[6] This is a powerful gift that further enhances Vos's tracking ability and discernment. He is even able to sense the emotions as well as the memories of the owners of certain objects, which can be a quite intense experience.

The various gifts of the Force used by Jedi remind me of St. Paul's explanation of charisms of the Holy Spirit:

> To each individual the manifestation of the Spirit is given for some benefit. To one is given through the Spirit the expression of wisdom; to another the expression of knowledge according to the same Spirit; to another faith by the same Spirit; to another gifts of healing by the one Spirit; to another mighty deeds; to another prophecy; to another discernment of spirits; to another varieties of tongues; to another interpretation of tongues. But one and the same Spirit produces all of these, distributing them individually to each person as he wishes. (1 Cor 12:7-11)

These Force gifts resemble what Catholics call gifts of the Holy Spirit, often focused upon in relation to the sacrament of Confirmation. Confirmation involves an unlocking of gifts and fruits of the Spirit in a way to better equip a Christian to fulfill his or her vocation and share the Gospel.

We might draw the comparison here between Force-sensitive younglings and baptized youth. Such youth have a connection to the Spirit by virtue of their baptism and its grace; however, they need additional nourishment to fully develop to their full spiritual potential. As younglings receive tutelage in the Jedi Temple and thereafter develop their Force abilities, so too baptized youth are formed within the Catholic fold and thereafter learn to identify and use their charisms.

St. Paul continues his discussion of charisms by noting that the highest of these gifts is love. He writes, "If I have the gift of prophecy, and comprehend all mysteries and all knowledge; if I have all faith so as to move mountains, but do not have love, I am nothing" (1 Cor 13:2). The Jedi focus on many of these gifts through the Force, and they are also committed to love. Anakin Skywalker discusses this dedication to love in a conversation with Padme. In *Episode II: Attack of the Clones* she says, "Are you allowed to love? I thought that was forbidden for a Jedi." Anakin replies, "Attachment is forbidden. Possession is forbidden. Compassion, which I would define as unconditional love, is central to a Jedi's life, so you might say that we're encouraged to love." At the essence of being a Jedi is love for all life, and other gifts in the Force come forth from that basic principle. Unfortunately, in this instance, Anakin's desires are not as pure as he would suggest, but his logic is sound. He equivocates on the word love, which should be altruistic for a Jedi, not romantic as he desires.

A special Force gift of the Jedi that relates to Catholicism is soul reading. Within Catholicism, we have examples of Saints who were able to "read" the souls of others, such at St. Pio of Pietrelcina who knew the sins of penitents confessing to him in the sacrament of Reconciliation. In *Star Wars* we see a hint of this in *The Phantom Menace* when Anakin is brought before the Jedi Council and they sense fear in him. It is a common practice of light and dark side Force users to detect the thoughts and feelings of others throughout the franchise. We further see this with Kylo Ren's interrogations in *The Force Awakens* and repeatedly by the Jedi Council in the prequels. While Kylo's method is highly invasive, the Council's seems to be more observational.

A special example of this gift, uniquely enhanced, is Yoda's special perception as revealed in the novel *Dark Disciple*. [SPOILER.] Speaking of Quinlan Vos, Yoda explains "'In his heart, darkness I found.' Yoda said sadly. 'Deep, secret, powerful. The history of items does the Force permit Vos to understand. The history of a *soul* does the Force permit *me* to understand.'"[7] While *Star Wars* is fiction, some of the most spectacular abilities of the Jedi are real gifts of the Spirit.

Commitment

The Jedi also require a strong commitment, as is necessary to be a Christian. Yoda's stern instruction in *The Empire Strikes Back* is memorable: "No, try not. Do, or do not. There is no try." We do not "try" to be a Christian. We may fail at times, but we must commit to it entirely and give ourselves to the Lord withholding nothing. Yoda highlights the gravity of being a Jedi when he teaches:

> A Jedi must have the deepest commitment, the most serious mind. This one [Luke], a long time

have I watched. All his life has he looked away, to the future, the horizon, never his mind on where he was, hm, what he was doing, hm. Adventure, heh, excitement, heh, a Jedi craves not these things. You are reckless. (*The Empire Strikes Back*)

According to Timothy Paul Jones, this commitment is the natural product of strong faith, just like for a Christian. He explains, "For the Jedi, however, to believe in the Force is not merely to admit the existence of the Force."[8] "Jedi Knights must believe so deeply in the larger world that they learn to live constantly in its power. Their beliefs must move beyond *mere acknowledgment* and give birth to *faithful commitment*," explains Jones.[9] Continuing he notes, "For the Jedi, faith is not only a way of *thinking about* the larger world but also a way of *living in* the larger world."[10] This applies to Christians as well.

Prayer and Meditation

Meditation and prayer are also values of the Jedi. Jesus tells the disciples, for example, that certain demons may only be driven out through prayer (Mk 9:14-29). In the prequels and *The Clone Wars*, Yoda and other Jedi are frequently in meditation. One of the repeated words to Luke during his training by Yoda is "concentrate." In the years after *Return of the Jedi*, Leia reveals some of the tutelage she received from Luke: "My brother taught me to center myself, to be mindful of what I am feeling. 'A cup to be filled up,' he says."[11] Leia is recognizing the importance of centered meditation, just as Yoda taught Luke he would know the good side from the bad when he is "calm, at peace, passive. Clear your mind of questions" (*The Empire Strikes Back*).

Catholics have a rich tradition of meditation, especially traditional devotions like Eucharistic Adoration, *Lectio Divina*, the Rosary, novenas, and the Stations of the Cross. In addition, Leia's reference to filling the cup resonates with Psalm 23:5, "My cup overflows." This has strong Christian meaning—we must be an empty cup, emptied of ourselves, so as to be filled up by the Lord. This relates to what John the Baptist says of Jesus, "He must increase; I must decrease" (Jn 3:30). A Jedi connects with the Force through meditation much like how a Christian connects with God through prayer—it is essential. Through Leia's meditation she is able to sense things, like the fact that the baby in her womb is a boy and how her mother, Padme, died.[12]

Sensing her son, Ben, Leia can also detect details about him in her womb:

> Him she can effortlessly feel inside her. Not just the way all mothers can feel the living creature within. But she can feel him with the invisible hands of the Force. With it she senses the margins of his burgeoning mind. She knows his mood; she can tell that he's healthy. He is less a human shaped thing and more a pulsing, living band of light. Light that sometimes dims, that sometimes is thrust through with a vein of darkness. She tells herself that it is normal. Luke said to her, "Leia, we all have that." He explained that the brighter the light, the darker the shadow.[13]

Sometimes through prayer and meditation the Spirit reveals things to us as well, such as truths about ourselves, how to handle a situation, and even greater insights for Catholic mystics.

Jedi Clergy

Speaking of the Jedi Order, their structure and even name resemble elements of Catholicism, which is filled with all sorts of religious orders, all with their own charisms of emphasis. Consider for example the Franciscans, Dominicans, Jesuits, Salesians, St. Teresa of Calcutta's Missionaries of Charity, and the order to which my father belongs—Glenmary Home Missioners. Each of these orders in the Church has its own focus, yet operates within the Church's overall mission of the salvation of souls. The Jedi Order is much like these religious orders, and it even has a hierarchy like the Catholic Church. Catholicism has the Bishop of Rome (the Pope) at the top, joined by the other bishops throughout the world. Below them in the hierarchy are the other clergy with a lesser degree of the sacrament of Holy Orders, the priests and then deacons. Finally, the laity constitute the remainder of the Christian family.

At the top of the Catholic hierarchy is the Pope, College of Cardinals, and Bishops. Few events in the Church are as significant as an international gathering of all the Bishops at an Ecumenical Council. This is the Church's Magisterium—the teaching authority of the Church. The home for the Church is Vatican City, which is the smallest, independent microstate in the world. The Jedi somewhat mirror this with the Jedi Temple, Jedi Council, and their Grand Master, Yoda.

Using the Force: *Star Wars* and Catholicism

The Temple is like Vatican City as *Ultimate Star Wars* notes:

> For thousands of years, the Jedi Temple has been the home of the Jedi Order on Coruscant. Part school and part monastery, the temple houses facilities for training and meditation, dormitories, medical centers, and archives that contain extensive data from across the galaxy.[14]

While the Jedi Council meets much more frequently than a Catholic ecumenical council (which is averaging one meeting per century), they enjoy the top authority among the Jedi Order. With some similarities to the Catholic Magisterium, "The circular High Council chamber holds a ring of 12 seats, one for each of the Jedi Masters who serve as Council members. Monitoring galactic events and contemplating the nature of the Force, the Council has final authority."[15] Just as the Pope has a special authority among his fellow bishops and the respect of the universal Church, Yoda has a special authority on the Council and respect among Jedi.

Not only do the Jedi practice obedience through their hierarchy, like Catholics, they also practice the other evangelical counsels of chastity and poverty shared by Catholic clergy and religious. It is unclear whether the discipline of celibacy has always been held for the Jedi, and how important it is for them. *Ultimate Star Wars* does reveal, "The Jedi Order prohibits Jedi from falling in love because such strong emotions can lead to the dark side."[16] In Catholicism we know that St. Paul was celibate of his own choice and suggested it for those who were able, in imitation of Christ (see 1 Cor

7:1, 8). It is also valued as a way to dedicate one's life fully to the Lord in exclusive love and service (see Mt 19:11-12).

However, celibacy was not mandatory for the first millennia of the Church's history and only became standard practice and a matter of law in the last approximately 1,000 years. This is an important discipline of the Church, yet it is not a teaching at so high a level that it could never change again. It is possible that Jedi of the Old Republic were also married, as we do not yet have much canon material about that era, as of this writing. It may happen that the Jedi of the future are also married, as Luke and Anakin seem to have saved the galaxy together as a result of their attachment to one another as son and father. A future Jedi order, or new order of virtuous force-wielders, may very well allow family bonds, including marriage.

There is great theological, spiritual, and practical value in celibate clergy. The same could be said of the Jedi. In *Attack of the Clones*, Anakin struggles between focusing on his duty and his interest in Padme. Throughout *The Clone Wars* series, Padme is often shown to be dedicated primarily to duty and Anakin second. All throughout their relationship such tension exists, which prevents them from giving themselves fully to either their marriage or their duty. The Jedi may have possessed higher wisdom after all, since Anakin's fall to the dark side is manipulated by Sidious using Anakin's attachment to saving Padme's life, despite constant warnings from various sources, as a means to corrupt him to evil.

We may also surmise that Jedi have at least an appreciation of poverty (through detachment) as well.

Catholic orders vary greatly on how strictly to observe this evangelical counsel, not only from order to order, but also within orders themselves. Varying degrees of this vow/promise are found from diocesan clergy to Franciscans, Jesuits, Carmelites, Cistercians, and so on. In any case, there is value placed on keeping one's life simple and even going as far as St. Francis of Assisi, who renounced all worldly things for the glory of God.

Like members of a religious order who may have access to considerable resources and material as a group, each individual Jedi has little to call their own other than a lightsaber, clothing, and perhaps very few personal belongings. Like a good Christian, this helps them keep focused on what is more important than worldly things. Interestingly, Count Dooku—having fallen from the Jedi order and become a dark Sith apprentice (known as Darth Tyranus) to Darth Sidious—is one of the most wealthy men in the *Star Wars* galaxy and a nobleman on his home world of Serenno.[17] His degree of personal wealth and power is held in sharp contrast to the Jedi who may command ships, legions of troops, and wield great authority during the Clone Wars, yet have little to call their own. All that they have is at the service of doing good for the galaxy and eliminating evil. For Dooku, however, his resources are privately held and used to fund much of the Separatist battle forces of the Clone Wars as part of an evil Sith plot.

Attachment

Another commitment of the Jedi is a life of non-attachment, which is true for Catholics as well. In *Catholicism*, Bishop Robert Barron reflects on the beatitudes and the crucifixion: "If you want beatitude (happiness), despise what Jesus despised on the cross and love what he loved on the cross. What did he despise on the cross but the four classical addictions?"[18] These include wealth/worldly goods, pleasure, power, and the esteem of others. "In the most dramatic way possible, therefore, the crucified Jesus demonstrates a liberation from the four principal temptations that lead us away from God."[19] Each of these are common attachments from which we need to be freed. Every denial of something is an embrace of another. Barron continues:

> But what did Jesus love on the cross? He loved the will of his Father. ... We can say that Jesus nailed to the cross is the very icon of liberty, for he is free from those attachments that would prevent him from attaining the true good which is doing the will of his Father.[20]

By detaching from the world, we are able to attach better to God. The Jedi commitment to non-attachment includes both material things and also romantic relationships. In this way they are able to focus on the Force, similar to how Catholics are to detach from temptations of the world and focus on God.

Jedi detachment has been misinterpreted at times, suggesting the Jedi are cold, uncaring, even merciless. Jedi Quinlan Vos clarifies, "Jedi aren't without emotion. We're allowed to grieve," much like Jesus wept at the death of his friend, Lazarus.[21] The *Dark Disciple* novel explains:

> The Jedi cultivated a practice of non-attachment, which had always served them well. Few understood, though, that while specific, individual bonds, such as romantic love or family were forbidden, the Jedi were not ashamed of compassion. All lives were precious, and when so many were lost in such a way, the Jedi felt the pain of it in the Force, as well as in their own hearts.[22]

We see this pain in the Force several times through the franchise. During the execution of Order 66 when the Jedi are being slaughtered, Yoda drops his cane to the ground and clasps himself in pain. Obi-Wan too senses the destruction of Alderaan, though less intensely, in *A New Hope*. In the *Ahsoka* novel, Ahsoka practices meditation and reaches out in the Force. Before the fall of the Republic, she could sense her fellow Jedi in the Force, especially her master, Anakin Skywalker; however, after Order 66, she only senses emptiness, which is mostly why she believes Anakin died in the Jedi purge.[23] A Jedi's ability to love is actually increased by his or her detachment from things standing between them and the Force, much like a Christian reaches greater perfection and love when united more closely to God.

Theological Virtues

Growth in virtue is also valued among the Jedi as in Catholicism. The three theological virtues of Faith, Hope, and Charity (Love), which have their source in God, may be seen in the Jedi with some modifications. While Catholics have faith in God and what he has revealed, the Jedi have faith in the Force and its will. The importance of faith is highlighted throughout the franchise, but my favorite is when Luke fails to lift his X-wing from the swamp in *The Empire Strikes Back*. Yoda is thereafter successful, and a disbelieving Luke gasps, "I don't, I don't believe it." To which Yoda replies, "That is why you fail." Faith is an essential component to using the Force and living as a Jedi. In *A New Hope*, according to Anker, "Lucas was concerned primarily with the necessity of belief in the numinous reality of the Force; that vital leap of faith allows Luke to destroy the Empire's Death Star."[24] Lucas himself explains, "That is what 'use the Force' is, it's a leap of faith, that there are mysteries and powers larger than we are and that you have to trust your feelings in order to access these things."[25]

Hope is a very strong theme in *Star Wars*. Beginning with Princess Leia's often quoted, "Help me, Obi-Wan Kenobi. You're my only hope," the idea reappears frequently. Episode IV was later titled *A New Hope* in reference to Luke, of whom Obi-Wan says, "That boy was our last hope," in *The Empire Strikes Back*. It is also the only word spoken by Leia in *Rogue One*. In the original trilogy, Luke's hope in the goodness of Anakin is what allows him to make his salvific sacrifice in *Return of the Jedi*. In season 3 of *The Clone Wars* [SPOILERS], while on Mortis with Ahsoka dead in his arms, Anakin pleads with the Father, who is holding his dying Daughter, to help him. Distraught, the Father says, "There is no hope," to which Anakin responds, "Yes there is. There's always hope!" In *Dark Disciple*, Yoda also affirms, "Hope, always, there is."[26] All of this is one type of hope, what Wilkinson calls "the hope of transformation and goodness now," and it is a strong theme in the franchise.[27]

The other type of hope is the theological virtue of hope. Catholics have hope in God's promise of eternal beatitude, or heaven, for those who die in a state of grace. For most of the Jedi Order prior to Order 66, the afterlife is more neutral than the eternal bliss hoped for by Christians. Every being transforms into the Force, and there is no alternative, like hell, about which to be concerned. There is no need for the theological virtue of hope, because everyone becomes one with the Force. The only exception is the rare Jedi who are able to retain their consciousness when they die, while becoming one with the Force: Qui-Gon, Obi-Wan, Yoda, Anakin, and presumably Luke following *The Last Jedi*. For the rest of the population, though, it is a moot point. Thus, while the idea of hope for a better existence in this life is strong in *Star Wars*, the theological virtue of hope is largely absent.

Charity or Love, the chief of all virtues, is the third theological virtue. The *Catechism* states: "We love God above all things for his own sake, and our neighbor as ourselves for the love of God."[28] God is always the initiator and loves us unconditionally first and foremost; our love back to God is a fitting response and is something we owe to him out of justice and thanksgiving. Thereafter, we love others, not because they deserve it (as we humans frequently do not deserve it), but because God loves them, God is present in them, and we are to imitate God who loves us unconditionally even though we are undeserving.

Jedi seem to emulate this virtue quite well. They have compassion on all life forms, probably because the Force emanates from all life, thus all life should be respected. An official source states, "The Jedi maintain that every life form in the galaxy, as well as the universe itself, is bound together and connected by an energy field called the Force."[29] Therefore, their compassion, care, and respect for all other life stems from their recognition of the Force itself. The way they view and appreciate their galaxy is colored by their relationship with the Force, as the way a Catholic encounters our created world is colored by our relationship with God. Anker notes, "What it is really about is radical love for all things, a posture [Force] devotees must take deeply into themselves if they wish to become full-fledged Jedis."[30] By the time we reach the end of the original trilogy, we have seen Luke display faith, hope, and love in a powerful, Christ-like way.

Human Virtues

Catholicism also emphasizes the four Cardinal Virtues as the primary ones from which all the other human virtues flow. Human virtues are all virtues other than the theological—they are ones we may acquire on our own through practice and habit. The four foundational Cardinal Virtues are prudence (being morally smart/wise), justice (giving others what they are due), temperance (moderation in our use of things), and fortitude (moral courage/strength).

Prudence is an essential characteristic of a Jedi and is taught at very young ages. Anakin's first encounter with his apprentice, Ahsoka Tano, in the Battle of Christophsis during the Clone Wars saw them teaming up to take out opponents. While Ahsoka was successful, she also committed errors of judgement and lacked prudence (among other virtues like humility).

Consequently, after the battle Anakin lightly rebuked her saying, "You're reckless little one. You never would have made it as Obi-Wan's padawan, but you might make it as mine."

Justice, temperance, and fortitude are also valued virtues in *Star Wars*. Jedi are expected to deal fairly with others and give them their due, including respect for all beings in the Force. They are expected to moderate their passions and practice temperance as well. A Jedi guilty of gluttony (an opposing vice of temperance) would be a silly thing to behold, indeed. It would be inconsistent with the self-control we have come to expect of the Jedi. Finally, fortitude is widely prized, as the Jedi are often required to do the right thing no matter the cost.

Perhaps the most powerful example of fortitude is Luke's moral courage in rejecting the Emperor's temptations to the dark side at the end of *Return of the Jedi*—even to the point of being willing to die for his virtue. This is what makes him a Jedi, as his father was before him. To save Luke from death, Vader subsequently offers himself in a sacrifice for his son that costs his own life. The title of *Episode VI*, "Return of the Jedi," may be interpreted as the return of the Jedi Order with Luke, but it may be more powerfully understood as the singular return of the Jedi Anakin Skywalker through this act of both fortitude and love.

Other human virtues are also emphasized, as we might expect from George Lucas, since he wished to guide youth in some moral instruction. We see honesty and integrity in the original trilogy as Han Solo's character matures and grows in virtue. The loyalty of various companions such as Chewbacca is undeniable. We later learned that Chewie had a life debt to Han for saving him at some point in the past, which is the initial root of his loyalty to him; however, it is clear they have formed a bond by the original trilogy beyond a mere legal contract. It has grown deeper, more covenantal.

Finally, forgiveness is displayed in a positive light. The struggle on Obi-Wan's face as he leaves the charred Anakin by the lava flow on Mustafar demonstrates how deeply Anakin's betrayal wounded him. The defeated Anakin screams at Obi-Wan, "I hate you!" Obi-Wan replies, "You were my brother, Anakin. I loved you." Not only does he avoid returning hate for hate, Obi-Wan must have come to forgive Anakin for his betrayal, because by *A New Hope*, he has a sense of serenity as he talks to Luke about Anakin's seduction by the dark side of the Force. He seems to find peace in believing the evil side of Anakin, namely Vader, killed the goodness of his friend he knew as Anakin Skywalker. Obi-Wan chooses forgiveness and peace to avoid the hatred that would lead him into darkness—a lesson Jesus taught by forgiving his executioners before he died.

Holy-One Kenobi

Obi-Wan is a superb example of virtue and character, with a developed ability to sense the will of the Force and to live in conformity with it. Obi-Wan was trained as a Jedi all his life, served on the Jedi Council in the final days of the Republic, survived Order 66, and spent nearly two decades on desolate Tatooine near Luke where he practiced meditation and learned the path to immortality. Caleb Grimes notes, "Obi-Wan undoubtedly comprehended that the busy lives of the Jedi in the Republic took them away from feeling the Force. This separation diminished their power and allowed evil to creep in virtually unseen."[31]

During this time he underwent deep character maturity as is evident in *A New Hope*. As Caleb Grimes puts it: "Obi-Wan does not resort to frantic movements or panicked responses, he listens to the Force and remains still. Only in stillness can one learn to hear its voice. Only when one hears its voice can one respond," writes Grimes.[32] Similarly, our busy lives make it difficult to hear God's voice, while quiet, meditative time can help us hear God better.

Why was Obi-Wan in the Jundland wastes when Luke was attacked, thereby being in a position to help, we may ask. Grimes posits:

> This was the Force directing him. ... Ben senses the Force moving even further, realizing that the time for action has finally arrived. ... He considers not only the plea for help from Princess Leia Organa, but also the way in which that message comes to him, and he to it.[33]

Obi-Wan has learned great patience and stillness, which have enhanced his ability to hear the Force and respond effectively to its promptings. Connecting this to Christianity, Grimes suggests:

> Being mindful of a succession of events, or things perceived as coincidences, is a good way to listen to God and become wiser; to learn to take those paths that he is directing you to take. Ben Kenobi learned to listen to the Force during all those years in the desert.[34]

Consequently, he resurfaces in *A New Hope* a much greater Jedi than in *Revenge of the Sith*, though his character was always impeccable.

Throughout the films and both of the animated series, Obi-Wan proves to be steadfast, trustworthy, dependable, of strong moral integrity, and yet he also has his weaknesses and shows his humanity. A Saint is merely a sinner in heaven, and Obi-Wan shows us a "realistic" human experience of life with all of its achievement, victory, loss, suffering, betrayal, passing on one's wisdom, and sacrifice for something greater. He is the embodiment of a Jedi. While not the most talented, brilliant, or powerful among the Jedi, his humility and virtue allow him to reach monumental achievement. For example, Anakin should have beaten him on Mustafar in their lightsaber battle, and Obi-Wan knew this. Consequently, Obi-Wan bided his time in the battle until he held the advantage; Obi-Wan fought defensively until he held the high ground. His victory was his humility over Anakin's pride, just as the tortoise beat the hare. At the end he chooses a degree of mercy and will not even take Anakin's life.

As much as Obi-Wan's relationship with Anakin provides a foil to highlight his virtue, Obi-Wan's relationship with Darth Maul is nearly as significant. Maul kills Obi-Wan's master, Qui-Gon Jinn; is immediately thereafter sliced in half by Obi-Wan; survives as a result of his hatred for Obi-Wan; and continues into a series of collisions with Obi-Wan throughout *The Clone Wars* and into *Rebels*. Throughout their interactions, Maul is full of hatred for Obi-Wan. [SPOILERS for *The Clone Wars* and *Rebels* follow in this section.] Maul kills Obi-Wan's only romantic interest in his life, Dutchess Satine Kryze of Mandalore, right in front of Obi-Wan, specifically to cause him intense agony. When Maul finally tracks Obi-Wan down at the end of *Rebels* Season 3, Obi-Wan harbors no animosity toward Maul even though Maul wants nothing more than to cause Obi-Wan as much suffering as possible.

Only when Maul realizes that Obi-Wan is hiding on Tatooine to protect "someone" is Obi-Wan forced to kill Maul in order to protect Luke Skywalker and his identity. As Maul dies, even after the terrible things Maul inflicted upon Obi-Wan, Obi-Wan holds him in his arms compassionately. He is the *Star Wars* epitome of forgiveness, humility, patience, and virtue. Perhaps as a result, Obi-Wan has the distinct honor (possibly by will of the Force) of being the first Jedi in a millennia to have successfully beaten two different Sith with three victories (Maul twice and Vader on Mustafar). Anakin would have nearly as significant success against the Sith, because he killed Count Dooku, defeated himself as Vader, and overthrew Emperor Palpatine. Not even Grand Master Yoda could tout as much success against the Sith in combat as Obi-Wan. Like us in the spiritual life, it is our humility and surrender that lead to Christ's victory in us, not our own power.

Grand Master

Speaking of Yoda, this Grand Master of the Jedi Order is also a superb example of virtue. Anker believes: "He echoes the prophecies of Isaiah about the coming Messiah. If Yoda is indeed who he seems to be, then the last are indeed first, the humble are exalted, and the obscure are the luminaries."[35] Yoda is the epitome of the unsuspecting, old sage from traditional myths, and his focus is on, among other things, growth in character. Anker further testifies: "Yoda's lessons for knighthood consist, not of better sword play or karate, but of humility, patience, tolerance, calm, and trust, a group of traits starkly opposed to those Luke manifests, and to some extent, venerates."[36]

Furthermore, Yoda resembles Jesus in the Beatitudes. Christ tells us not only to avoid murder but the root of it—hate—as well. Similarly, Jesus taught not only to avoid adultery, but also to avoid even the thought of lust in our hearts. Yoda constantly reminds his pupils to avoid anger, fear, hate, and aggression, which are the beginning of starting down the "dark path."[37] "In the psycho-moral realm of the Force in *Star Wars*, and the New Testament, the deed inexorably follows the thought; morality is measured by spirit as much as by deed," explains Anker.[38] This explains why Yoda's tutelage penetrates deeply. Like Christianity, he understands the importance of the desires and battles of the heart which precede the actions. Even the Sith recognize this. Foreseeing when Vader may turn on him, Sidious asks Vader, "Do you think treachery begins in the deed, my friend?" to which Vader responds, "No, it begins in the thoughts."[39]

In a profound comparison of Yoda to Vader, McDowell writes:

> *The difference between Yoda and Vader has to do with different conceptions of power and the self.* For Vader, power is the power of force and the right of might; for Yoda, power has to do with the virtues of wisdom, self-control, and just living. For Vader, the self is to be exalted at others' expense, while Yoda is a servant of the Force, and correspondingly a servant of all living things.[40]

With this we turn our attention from the Jedi to the Sith.

Using the Force: *Star Wars* and Catholicism

[1] *Ultimate Star Wars* (New York: DK Penguin Random House, 2015), 20.

[2] Ibid, 89.

[3] E. K. Johnston, *Star Wars: Ahsoka*, Audiobook narrated by Ashley Eckstein (Random House Audio, 2016), approximately 4:34:00.

[4] *Ultimate Star Wars*, 123.

[5] Kevin Hearne, *Star Wars: Heir to the Jedi*, Audiobook narrated by Marc Thompson (Random House Audio, 2015), 3:36:45.

[6] *Ultimate Star Wars*, 42.

[7] Christie Golden, *Star Wars: Dark Disciple*, Audiobook narrated by Marc Thompson (Random House Audio, 2015), 9:02:24.

[8] Timothy Paul Jones, *Finding God in a Galaxy Far, Far Away: A Spiritual Exploration of the Star Wars Saga* (Sisters, OR: Multnomah, 2005), 47.

[9] Ibid.

[10] Ibid., 47-48.

[11] Chuck Wendig, *Star Wars Aftermath: Life Debt*, Audiobook narrated by Marc Thompson. (Random House Audio, 2016), approximately 2:32:34.

[12] Ibid., approximately 7:24:00 and 12:05:55.

[13] Ibid., 9:42:25.

[14] *Ultimate Star Wars*, 170.

[15] Ibid.

[16] Ibid, 38.

[17] Simon Beecroft and Pablo Hidalgo, *Star Wars Character Encyclopedia*, 2nd ed. (New York: DK Penguin Random House, 2016) 57.

[18] Robert Barron, *Catholicism: A Journey to the Heart of the Faith* (New York: Image, 2011), 45.

[19] Ibid, 46.

[20] Ibid.

[21] Golden, 3:27:54.

[22] Ibid., 12:32.

[23] E. K. Johnston, *Star Wars: Ahsoka*, Audiobook narrated by Ashley Eckstein (Random House Audio, 2016).

[24] Roy M. Anker, *Catching Light: Looking for God in the Movies* (Grand Rapids, MI: William B. Eerdmans Publishing Company, 2004), 228.

[25] Bill Moyers, *The Mythology of Star Wars with George Lucas and Bill Moyers* (Public Affairs Television, Inc., 1999), https://vimeo.com/groups/183185/videos/38026023 (accessed 21 July 2017).

[26] Golden, 14:08).

[27] Wilkinson, 95.

[28] *Catechism of the Catholic Church*, 2d ed. (Citta del Vaticano: Libreria Editrice Vaticana, 1997), § 1822.

[29] *Ultimate Star Wars*, 11.

[30] Anker, 228.

[31] Caleb Grimes, *Star Wars Jesus: A Spiritual Commentary on the Reality of the Force* (Enumclaw, WA: WinePress Publishing, 2007), 27.

[32] Ibid.

[33] Ibid., 28.

[34] Ibid.

[35] Anker, 230.

[36] Ibid..

[37] Ibid., 231.

[38] Ibid., 235.

[39] Paul S. Kemp, *Star Wars: Lords of the Sith*, Audiobook narrated by Jonathan Davis (Random House Audio, 2015), 7:22:50.

[40] John C. McDowell, *The Gospel According to Star Wars: Faith, Hope, and the Force* (Louisville, Westminster John Knox Press, 2007), 119.

Chapter 6: Sith

"The Sith and the Jedi are similar in almost every way."
— Chancellor Palpatine (*Revenge of the Sith*)

The Sith are an ancient order of dark side Force users in opposition to the Jedi. George Lucas explains that the Sith "'were greedy and self-centered and they all wanted to take over, so they killed each other. ... [T]hat is the antithesis of a symbiotic relationship,' and is instead a 'cancer' that eventually kills the host."[1] An example of the cancerous malignance of the dark side may be seen in the *Tarkin* novel. We learn that the Jedi Temple of Coruscant, which Sidious would eventually turn into the Imperial Palace, was actually built upon a Sith shrine.[2] The effects of this are explained in the following:

> Even the most powerful of the Jedi believed that the power inherent in the shrine had been neutralized and successfully capped. In truth,

that power had seeped upward and outward since its entombment, infiltrating the hallways and rooms above and weakening the Jedi order much as the Sith masters themselves had secretly infiltrated the corridors of political power and toppled the Republic. … Even Vader was unaware of the shrine's existence, but it was here that [Vader and Sidious] would one day work together the way that Sidious and Plagueis had, to coax the dark side its final secrets.[3]

Sidious later talks about needing two Sith at the dark side shrine with one acting as "bait" for the dark side so that the other can extract its "final secrets."[4] It seems the dark side is being manipulated by the Sith, even fought against, while the Jedi connect with the light and work with it, especially when calm, at peace, and passive. This seems much like angels working with God, contrasted with demons rebelling against God and living in tension amongst themselves. The Jedi are like Catholicism working with God, and the Sith are like practitioners of evil, including manipulation of demonic spirits to do their will—spirits that may come back to burn them.[5]

Rule of Two

As we learn in *The Clone Wars*, Darth Bane is the sole survivor of the ancient wars among the Sith. He is still remembered by the Sith as the one who instituted the "Rule of Two"—one master, one apprentice. This tenuous relationship usually ended with the apprentice killing the master. [SPOILERS for the rest of this section.] In *Lords of the Sith*, we learn about a Sith relationship:

> The relationship between Sith apprentice and Master was symbiotic but in a delicate balance. An apprentice owed his master loyalty; a master owed his apprentice knowledge and must show only strength. But the obligations were reciprocal and contingent. Should either fail in his obligation, it was the duty of the other to destroy him. The Force required it.[6]

Reflecting on this relationship, the novel shortly thereafter mentions, "Perhaps Vader would attempt to kill his master one day. Sith apprentices ordinarily did, they must if they were trained well…both master and apprentice knew this."[7]

This theme continues throughout the novel. After walking in the jungle of Ryloth with the Emperor and two guards, Vader meditated and revealed to Sidious:

> "[I] saw deaths and faces from my past, the events that led me to this moment. I see them frequently when I consider the destiny the Force has for me."… For a moment, caught up in the after effects of his vision, Vader wondered what it would be like to face his Master in battle. To take his small, frail body in his hands, lift it from the ground and… he cut off the thoughts, but his Master had sensed them, for his face split in a dark smile. "I see you, apprentice." "And I see you Master. You think I long for the past when I see it in visions, but you're wrong. I don't long for it, I think of it and the man I was then and

regard it with contempt, and the only thing that makes it tolerable to ponder is that it ends with me here in this armor, with you. I feel no longing. I feel no regret. My memories feed my anger, and my anger feeds my strength, and so am I able to serve you and the Force better. Your doubt is unwarranted and... angers me."[8]

This "understanding" between the two of them continues, because Vader's thoughts repeatedly return to rebellion, just as a demon is locked in the consequences of its rebellious nature. Later in the story, Vader, Sidious, and two Royal Guards are under attack by a horde of hundreds of huge insect-like creatures native to Ryloth called lyleks. Seeing the Emperor battling dozens of them below, Vader thinks for a moment, "His master dead; Vader ruling the Empire; the Galaxy unconstrained by the leash of an old man. He killed the thought," and rejoined his master, battling off the lyleks.[9] Once Vader is on the ground with Sidious, the Emperor says to him, "Enjoyable, no? Did you consider allowing me to die to realize your own ambitions?' Vader didn't even attempt to lie. 'I did, but only for a moment.' 'Good, very good,'" replies Sidious.[10] The way Sidious tests Vader and others continues throughout the novel.

In fact, the entire *Lords of the Sith* novel is ultimately a ruse. Sidious allowed himself and Vader to fall into a compromising and life-threatening situation in order not only to draw out the rebellious Free Ryloth Movement (getting them to expend all of their resources), but perhaps more importantly to test Vader's commitment to the dark side, his strength, and his ability to overcome the residual good within.[11] We can witness from these examples how awful a Sith relationship truly is. It totally lacks concern, love, and respect for the other, merely being a contractual power play until one kills the other.

Evil Personified

As a theme, used especially with the Sith, George Lucas shows that evil is not something foreign to us, but it is something with which we grapple inside ourselves. This is the primary lesson Luke "fails" in the cave on Dagobah; "the enemy lies as much within us as without, and that poses a daunting moral and spiritual challenge," writes Anker.[12] Consider further the character design of Darth Maul, who evokes resemblance to Satan and evil icons from many cultures. Lucas wanted him to appear human-like so that "we could identify with him, because he's not a monster we cannot identify with, he's the evil within us."[13] Lucas explains, "The film is ultimately about the dark side and the light side, and those sides are designed around compassion and greed, and we all have those two sides of us, and that we have to make sure that those two sides of us are in balance."[14] *Star Wars* highlights the importance of recognizing the reality of good and evil, and our ability to choose between the two in our lives, thereby deciding our character.

The Sith Lord, Darth Sidious, known also as Emperor Sheev Palpatine, bears a striking character resemblance to Satan, though less a visual one compared to Darth Maul. The *Catechism of the Catholic Church* quotes John 8:44 and Revelation 12:9 describing Satan as, "'A murderer from the beginning, ...a liar and the father of lies,' Satan is 'the deceiver of the whole world.'"[15] The way Sidious grooms and deceives Anakin throughout the prequels and *The Clone Wars* is demonic. As McDowell notes, "Sidious's rise to political power...is made particularly possible because he is able to manufacture situations beneficial to himself by exploiting others' *self-concern*."[16]

For example, in *Attack of the Clones* Palpatine counsels Anakin, "You don't need guidance, Anakin. In time you will learn to trust your feelings. Then you will be invincible. I have said it many times, you are the most gifted Jedi I have ever met." Palpatine knows just what to say to plant seeds of darkness in Anakin's mind. Timothy Paul Jones suggests, "The ruler of the Galactic Republic has confirmed what Anakin has long suspected—that he doesn't need guidance, that he needs only to pursue the power his heart so deeply covets."[17]

Palpatine continues to fan the flame, "I see you becoming the greatest of all the Jedi, Anakin. Even more powerful than Master Yoda." Jones notices, "When Anakin Skywalker leaves the chancellor's office, the boy is buoyant, sailing on the wild currents of his own pride."[18] That is a dangerous condition for someone as inherently powerful and volatile as Anakin Skywalker, and that is precisely what Palpatine intends to manipulate to his advantage. The old adage states, "Pride cometh before a fall," and this is certainly true for Anakin. McDowell notes, "According to Aristotle, the cardinal flaw the tragic hero suffers from is *hubris*, and usually this is translated as 'pride' or 'arrogance,'" certainly weaknesses of Anakin.[19] Prophetically, while walking through the Jedi Temple, Grand Master Yoda notices that arrogance is "a flaw more and more common among Jedi. Too sure of themselves they are, even the older, more experienced ones" (*Attack of the Clones*).[20]

Obi-Wan tells Padme in *Revenge of the Sith* that Anakin "was deceived by a lie. We all were. It appears that the Chancellor [Sidious] is behind everything, including the war." Darth Sidious, like Satan, "masquerades as an angel of light" (2 Cor 11:14). He twists Anakin's allegiance by telling him the power of the dark side can prevent Padme, his wife, from dying, and they can rule the galaxy for "the good of all" (*Revenge of the Sith*).

People usually do not choose evil when is it blatantly obvious to them. Instead, they choose the good they think exists in doing evil, often rationalizing sinful actions to make them seem justified. In the case of Padme's potential death in childbirth, as Anakin has been dreaming, Sidious appeals to the good of saving Padme. The problem here is the means through which Anakin must achieve his goal—he must embrace the dark side and become a Sith, betraying all that is good. Sidious is tempting Anakin by offering him good things, like peace and order in the galaxy and saving Padme's life, much like the serpent tempting Adam and Eve with the fruit.

Sidious deceives Anakin in a subtle way; he tells Anakin only through the dark side can he save Padme from dying, as Darth Plagueis was supposedly able to do. However, only after Anakin has turned to the dark side and pledged himself to Sidious does Sidious admit he has not yet discovered how to prevent people from dying as Plagueis supposedly could. He suggests that together they may be able to achieve this in time—it is an empty promise. This echoes the Rite of Baptism where we reject Satan, all his works, and all of his empty promises. Sidious promises Anakin something he cannot give in order to get Anakin to turn evil, just as demons do to us. Temptations are all empty promises.

Sidious also causes Anakin to doubt the good of the Jedi, much like the serpent caused Eve to doubt God in the Garden of Eden. The serpent told Eve should she eat of the fruit of the tree, "You certainly will not die! No, God knows well that the moment you eat of it your eyes will be opened and you will be like gods who know what is good and what is bad" (Gn 3:4-5). Sidious made Anakin doubt the Jedi by calling into question their decision to have Anakin spy on Palpatine—a decision that already shook Anakin's trust in the Jedi Council. Here Sidious, like Satan, points to the faults of the generally good Jedi in order to compromise Anakin's trust in them. Such actions are typical of Satan and demons, as well as human predators, who will isolate a victim from those who truly care about him or her in order to abuse the victim. Obi-Wan makes Anakin's transition to the dark side clear when he tells him, "You have allowed this Dark Lord to twist your mind until now, until now you have become the very thing you swore to destroy" (*Revenge of the Sith*).

Corrupted Light, Darkness Is

The use of the dark side of the Force is "unnatural" as Sidious himself hints during the opera scene in *Revenge of the Sith*, further drawing the connection to Catholic theology. As discussed earlier when considering why the Force is not dualistic, we noted that the true nature of the force seems to be the light side. The dark side is not an equal yet opposite reality to the light side, like Yin and Yang of Taoism, but rather the distortion, the twisting, of the light side. This is precisely what we see in Christianity. Only God creates, and what God creates is good. Agents of free will (i.e., humans and angels) are capable of using their choice to follow the will of God and work in harmony with creation or to choose their own will, opposed to God's will, and corrupt the natural order established by God. Thus, God didn't create demons any more than he created murderers or rapists. Rather, he created angels and people (made in his image and likeness) who possess free will and are capable of distorting their good nature into a corrupt, fallen state.

Anakin is the most obvious example we have of this corruption by the dark side; however, it seems every Sith (so far in canon, at least) was once good and warped to evil. We know very little about Darths Bane, Plagueis, and Sidious. Nonetheless, we know that Darths Maul, Tyranus (Dooku), and Vader were all once good, or relatively good, and were twisted to become Sith. Maul was a Zabrak from Dathomir who was the son of Mother Talzin.[21] Even though Zabrak look evil with their horns, they are not an evil species. Eeth Koth, after all, is a Zabrak Jedi. It does not bode well for Maul that he was the son of a dark witch, as that may have had an effect on his nurtured goodness, but that is hardly his fault and does not affect his inherent goodness. An official source states, "Darth Sidious takes a male Zabrak infant named Maul from Dathomir and raises him as his apprentice."[22] Maul has been corrupted since infancy by the most twisted villain in *Star Wars* lore, as well as having been the son of a dark witch mother. His situation is poor from the outset, but it remains likely he was inherently good.

Darth Tyranus, more popularly known as Count Dooku, was a Jedi trained under Master Yoda who "Became disillusioned with the Jedi Order and thirsted for greater power."[23] He took on his hereditary position as Count of Serenno, one of the wealthiest individuals in the galaxy. He clearly started on the light before falling into darkness. [SPOILERS follow for the rest of the section.] Similarly, even the Grand Inquisitor in *Rebels* is revealed to have been a Jedi Temple Guard turned to the dark side.[24]

In *Star Wars*, we also see Sith and dark side users switch from evil to good. Again, Anakin Skywalker is the best known, but the life of Asajj Ventress highlights the fall of a person into darkness and back from evil as well as anyone in *Star Wars* canon. According to *Ultimate Star Wars*, Ventress's "mother is forced to trade Ventress to the criminal Hal'Sted to protect their clan" when she is young.[25] Working as a slave, she is later discovered by "Jedi Ky Narec [who] observes Ventress's Force sensitivity and trains her until he is murdered."[26] This training lasted a decade, and when Narec died, she was overcome with anger.[27] Discovering her in this condition, Count Dooku takes her as his assassin apprentice. Later, when Sidious senses "her growing strength in the Force," he commands Dooku to kill her.[28] She survived and returned to the Nightsisters on Dathomir and was initiated into their clan with their witchcraft and dark magick. When they were slaughtered, she was on her own again, having suffered much to feed her anger. Asajj Ventress took work as a bounty hunter and was able to make her way back from the evil of the dark side, though she still dabbled in it to a degree. There is some problematic moral ambiguity here, as we cannot dabble in darkness and still remain pure.

When Asajj teamed up with Jedi Quinlan Vos in *Dark Disciple* to kill Count Dooku, she is convinced Vos must learn the dark side to defeat Dooku, and she wishes to train him. In order to convince Vos, she feeds him half-truths:

> Ventress realized that she had cemented his trust in her, given him a personal vendetta against Dooku [when she lied and told him Dooku killed Vos's master when, in truth, Ventress was the one to kill him], and sparked resentment toward the [Jedi] Council, all with a few, well-chosen words. Such was the treacherous power of the dark side."[29]

Ventress learned how to manipulate from Dooku and was using it on Vos.

Ventress and Vos come to their relationship from dark and light backgrounds, which are obvious in their interactions. Vos eventually gives in to Ventress's training in the dark side, which is revealed at the end of the novel as having been a grave mistake. Ventress maintains she is able to use the dark side without falling into it—a rare and dangerous way to approach the dark side. She explains to him that the Nightsisters "grow up steeped in [the Dark Side], but we can use it as a tool and stay ourselves unlike the Sith. That balance is what you must learn."[30] Vos later comments:

> "The Jedi have always taught that the dark side is a quick and easy path."

"You must be cautious how far down that quick and easy path you go," she warned. "Now that you've tapped into it, it can consume you. It is a delicate balance to strike—being free enough to feed from it but remaining your own master."
"Like you did,"
"I fought my way back; I almost didn't make it."[31]

Later Ventress summarizes, "You need to tap into the darkness but not let it consume you."[32] Indeed, this is a compromising situation as the course of the novel reveals.

Later in the novel Vos is being consumed by the dark side and is in great peril. As Ventress is trying to save Vos and bring him back to the light, Vos tries to convince her of his plan to continue using dark power for good ends. Ventress lifts the shroud of dark lies and beautifully reveals the consequences of a life in the dark side:

> "What kind of life will that be, Quinlan?" Her voice broke. "The kind where we're slaves to our hatred, our rage? That's what the dark side made me; that's what it does. Nothing is ever enough. You get more and more, but you're never happy. It's a trap, baited with all the things you want most. That life, it's not worth living. … I already left that behind. You can too. You have a choice."[33]

Vos continues to wrestle with his options at that point, but Ventress further articulates, "Fear and disaster, an existence that could never be called living but merely crawling about in a shell of flesh that had no spark of joy—that too could be the future. ... Burning vengeance that only increased the hunger for more."[34]

Dooku, who was present throughout this whole conversation, strikes out at Vos with Force lightning to kill him but hits Ventress who leaps to save Vos. As Ventress lay dying from the lightning, Vos attacks and defeats Dooku who says,

> "Do it. ... Go on, take your revenge..." The count still smiled, still anticipated the final step that would turn Vos irrevocably to the dark side. "I am not your kind," Vos said, his voice thick. "I do not feed off vengeance." Truth was quiet. It did not need to shout or to demand. It simply existed. "I am a Jedi."[35]

In this intense moment, Vos heeds Ventress's warnings and chooses the light, just as she did.

In their final moments together as Asajj Ventress dies, we see truths of our faith articulated well in Ventress as she speaks to Vos:

> "I am proud of you for what you did over there. You chose loving me instead of hating him... best choice you ever made."
> "It was," he agreed. He swallowed hard. "Asajj you were right. I did fall to the dark side, and I've been there this whole time. I just, I didn't know."
> "You lied to yourself," Ventress whispered. "That's why I couldn't tell."
> "I love you, and I never stopped, not for a moment."

"I know," Ventress said. "But you did stop lying." She shuddered deeply. Vos felt his heart crack. Her fingers dug into his arm tightly, and her gaze bored into his. "Now remember, you always have a choice to be better. You always have a choice to...to pick the right path." She smiled sadly. "Even if that choice comes a little too late." ... "And always remember that I loved you, with all of my heart." ...
"Please, please don't."
"You must let me go, my Love," Ventress said, her voice so gentle, so tender, and she smiled lovingly. "It's the Jedi way." And she was gone.[36]

Vos, when interrogated by the Jedi Council after the whole experience, can only sob and repeat, "She saved me."[37] As Vos and Kenobi lay Ventress's body to rest, Vos says, "I'm on the path, Asajj. You bought my chance with blood, and I won't waste it."[38] His words would be appropriate in the mouth of a Christian appreciative of Christ's bloody sacrifice on our behalf.

All of these examples further illustrate that darkness is a corruption of light. Maul, Dooku, Vader, Ventress, and Vos were all good turned evil, and three of them came back from the darkness to the light. Ventress testified to how awful it is to be in darkness, the emptiness and lifelessness she experienced. Even for those in the darkest of places, light and hope always remain, much the way faith, hope, and love endure despite the greatest of evils.

Feeling Like Sith

Fear, anger, hate, suffering, and pain are all qualities of the dark side and the Sith. These qualities are in stark contrast to Catholic virtues and values. In the first minute of the novel *Lords of the Sith*, we get a glimpse into the dark side psyche of Darth Vader:

> Vader completed his meditation and opened his eyes. His pale, flame-savaged face stared back at him from out of the reflective black transparisteel of his pressurized mediation chamber. Without the neural connection to his armor, he was conscious of the stumps of his legs, the ruin of his arms, the perpetual pain in his flesh. He welcomed it. Pain fed his hate and hate fed his strength. Once, as a Jedi he had meditated to find peace. Now he meditated to sharpen the edges of his anger. He stared at his reflection a long time. His injuries had deformed his body, left it broken, but they perfected his spirit, strengthening his connection to the Force. Suffering had birthed insight. … From within a sea of scars, his gaze simmered with controlled, harnessed fury. … He welcomed the spikes of pain when the helmet's neuro-needles stabbed into the flesh of his skull and the base of his spine, unifying his body, mind, and armor to form an interconnected unit. … He never felt more connected to the Force than when his fury burned.[39]

We see here the degree to which Vader embraced his pain, hate, and suffering to fuel his dark side abilities. Looking through his perspective helps us better understand how remarkably twisted dark lords become, the extent of his downfall, and the magnitude of his conversion in *Return of the Jedi*. Moments later in *Lords of the Sith*, we receive additional information on how these emotions play into Vader's concept of power, and what motivates him:

> Yoda once had told him that fear led to hate and hate to suffering, but Yoda had been wrong. Fear was a tool used by the strong to cow the weak. Hate was the font of true strength. Suffering was not the result of the rule of the strong over the weak, order was. By its very existence the Force mandated the rule of the strong over the weak. The force mandated order. The Jedi had never seen that and so they'd misunderstood the Force and been destroyed. But Vader's master saw it, Vader saw it, and so they were strong, and so they ruled.[40]

This discussion of order by fear segues into the topic of power.

Power Play

The Sith are obsessed with power. "Siths' self-centeredness is expressed in terms of the menacing *power and control over others*," explains McDowell.[41] This is decidedly worldly, which is an idea opposed to God's kingdom here on earth. In Obi-Wan and Maul's final encounter from *Rebels* season 3, Obi-Wan tells Maul, "If you define yourself by your power to take life, the desire to dominate, to possess, then you have nothing."

We are to be focused on what is above, not things of this world, especially power. Sidious's deepest desires are revealed in the *Tarkin* novel:

> Eventually the dark side would grant him infallible foresight, but until such time future events would remain just out of clear sight, clouded by possibilities, the unremitting swirlings of the Force. ... He would not allow himself to be sidetracked from his goal of unlocking the secrets many of the Sith masters before him had sought, the means to harness the dark side to reshape reality itself. In effect, to fashion a universe of his own creation. Not mere immortality of the sort Plagueis had lusted after but influence of the ultimate sort.[42]

Sidious was after the most profound power he could imagine, yet it was still of the physical realm. Even though Plagueis wanted immortality, only light side users could attain it. Even though Sidious wanted the power to create a universe of his own, he would die at the hands of his apprentice, burned by the dark fire he lit and stoked. Conversely, the humble Jedi, who do not seek such great things, may be graced with immortality. We ought to remember, "The last will be first, and the first will be last," (Mt 20:16) and "Whoever exalts himself will be humbled; but whoever humbles himself will be exalted" (Mt 23;12).

A superb example of Sidious's Satan-like character, the differences between Jedi and Sith, and an exploration of Sidious's lust for power is the discussion of Palpatine and Anakin at the Galaxies Opera House in *Revenge of the Sith*:

PALPATINE: The Sith and the Jedi are similar in almost every way, including their quest for greater power.

ANAKIN: The Sith rely on their passion for their strength. They think inwards, only about themselves.

PALPATINE: And the Jedi don't?

ANAKIN: The Jedi are selfless . . . they only care about others.

PALPATINE: (continuing) Did you ever hear the tragedy of Darth Plagueis "the wise"?

ANAKIN: No.

PALPATINE: I thought not. It's not a story the Jedi would tell you. It's a Sith legend. Darth Plagueis was a Dark Lord of the Sith, so powerful and so wise he could use the Force to influence the midi-chlorians to create life. He had such a knowledge of the dark side, he could even keep the ones he cared about from dying.

ANAKIN: He could actually save people from death?

PALPATINE: The dark side of the Force is a pathway to many abilities some consider to be unnatural.

ANAKIN: What happened to him?

Using the Force: *Star Wars* and Catholicism

> PALPATINE: He became so powerful... the only thing he was afraid of was losing his power, which eventually, of course, he did. Unfortunately, he taught his apprentice everything he knew, then his apprentice killed him in his sleep. It's ironic. He could save others from death, but not himself.
>
> ANAKIN: Is it possible to learn this power?
>
> PALPATINE: Not from a Jedi.

Sidious is a manipulating tempter like Satan, capable of luring Anakin into his snare and making him subservient to his will.

Sidious/Palpatine's manipulation goes quite impressively beyond Anakin to the entire galaxy. He is behind the orchestration of the Separatists (formally known as the Confederacy of Independent Systems), who are under the leadership of Count Dooku, his apprentice. Years earlier he took secret control of the clone army on Kamino after Jedi Master Sifo-Dyas went against the Jedi Council's orders and had them grown due to Sifo-Dyas's belief that a war was coming and the Republic would need troops. He made sure the clones had a chip implanted in their brains during early development to ensure strict obedience to Order 66. After the start of the war, Sidious/Palpatine played both sides and kept the Republic in a state of fear and doubt, while using his control to position himself for success and more power in the midst of the crises he further orchestrated. His manipulations are the *modus operandi* of the Sith. Asajj Ventress recalls this about Count

Dooku: "This is what Dooku did, it was how he controlled people. He planted doubts in the soil he found fertile, and the darkness took root from those doubts."⁴³ The depth of Sidious/Palpatine's planning is immense and remarkably effective.

We may use these examples as warnings in our own spiritual lives. The Emperor said to Luke, "In time, you will call me Master." Matthew 6:24 warns, "No one can serve two masters." Grimes instructs, "It is eternally and universally important whom we call Master, and both God and Satan want us to call them by that name and put them in that position in our lives. Of course, there are lesser masters that we opt for all the time."⁴⁴ The point here is for us to take an inventory of our souls, to see where our heart's devotion truly lies. Are we unreservedly committed to God—surrendering power over our lives to him—or have we sold our allegiance to a lesser creature or thing and distanced ourselves from God?

---

[1] John C. McDowell, *The Gospel According to Star Wars: Faith, Hope, and the Force* (Louisville, Westminster John Knox Press, 2007), 46.

[2] James Luceno, *Star Wars: Tarkin,* Audiobook narrated by Euan Morton (Random House Audio, 2014), approximately 3:37:30.

[3] Ibid., approximately 3:37:30.

[4] Ibid., 3:44:00.

[5] Ibid., approximately 3:44:00.

[6] Paul S. Kemp, *Star Wars: Lords of the Sith,* Audiobook narrated by Jonathan Davis (Random House Audio, 2015), 53:23.

[7] Ibid., 54:14.

[8] Ibid., 7:28:06.

[9] Ibid., 8:38:40.

[10] Ibid., 8:40:20.

[11] Ibid., 10:54:30.

[12] Roy M. Anker, *Catching Light: Looking for God in the Movies* (Grand Rapids, MI: William B. Eerdmans Publishing Company, 2004), 231.

13 Bill Moyers, *The Mythology of Star Wars with George Lucas and Bill Moyers* (Public Affairs Television, Inc., 1999), https://vimeo.com/groups/183185/videos/38026023 (accessed 21 July 2017).

14 Ibid.

15 *Catechism of the Catholic Church*, 2d ed. (Citta del Vaticano: Libreria Editrice Vaticana, 1997), § 2852.

16 McDowell, 47.

17 Timothy Paul Jones, *Finding God in a Galaxy Far, Far Away: A Spiritual Exploration of the Star Wars Saga* (Sisters, OR: Multnomah, 2005), 64.

18 Ibid., 65.

19 McDowell, 72.

20 Ibid.

21 *Ultimate Star Wars* (New York: DK Penguin Random House, 2015), 36.

22 Ibid., 25.

23 "Count Dooku," *Star Wars Databank*, http://www.starwars.com/databank/count-dooku (accessed 8 July 2017).

24 E. K. Johnston, *Star Wars: Ahsoka*, Audiobook narrated by Ashley Eckstein (Random House Audio, 2016), approximately 6:26:00.

25 *Ultimate Star Wars*, 82.

26 Ibid.

27 Christie Golden, *Star Wars: Dark Disciple*, Audiobook narrated by Marc Thompson (Random House Audio, 2015), 3:27:54.

28 *Ultimate Star Wars*, 82.

29 Christie Golden, *Star Wars: Dark Disciple*, Audiobook narrated by Marc Thompson (Random House Audio, 2015),3:46:48.

30 Golden, 3:50:25.

31 Ibid., 4:48:00.

32 Ibid., 6:44:40.

33 Ibid., 10:40:40.

34 Ibid., 10:42:19.

35 Ibid., 10:43:30.

36 Ibid., 10:49:42.

37 Ibid., 10:56:02.

38 Ibid., 11:04:25.

39 Kemp, 0:00:36.

40 Ibid., 4:08.

41 McDowell, 47.

42 Luceno, *Tarkin*, 8:47:15.

[43] Golden, 10:35:15.

[44] Caleb Grimes, *Star Wars Jesus: A Spiritual Commentary on the Reality of the Force* (Enumclaw, WA: WinePress Publishing, 2007), 167.

Chapter 7: Anakin Skywalker

"I will be the most powerful Jedi ever."
– Anakin Skywalker (*Attack of the Clones*)

Following our exploration of the Jedi and Sith, it is appropriate to take a look at the central character of the prequel and original film series—Anakin Skywalker. Surrounding Anakin are a majority of the most significant events in the franchise. Our first exposure to him (in original order) is unbeknown to us, as he is shrouded as Darth Vader in *A New Hope*. All we have are shadows of truth from his past as revealed through Obi-Wan to Luke and the realization that Anakin was Luke's father, a Jedi Knight. Anakin's story shows us the depth of human virtue, vice, suffering, choice, and ultimately triumph of good over evil with his redemption. Anakin's story is a Catholic story.

Prophecy

Echoing messianic prophecies from our world, Anakin is born of a woman (Shmi Skywalker) who was without relation to man at the time of Anakin's conception. Whether Shmi was a virgin before Anakin's conception is unknown, though we do know that she marries Cliegg Lars later, so she is not likely to have remained a perpetual virgin like Mary. Nonetheless, the birth of a boy without a father must be an intentional parallel in *Star Wars* to the Christian messiah—Jesus Christ. It tells the audience this boy is of great significance. Of course, the audience already knows the conclusion to Anakin's life, but we are curious to learn how such a gifted and selfless slave boy could rise and fall in what is an authentic tragedy.

Anakin's conception is thought to be the result of the midi-chlorians and the Force, as Qui-Gon Jinn reveals to the Jedi Council in *The Phantom Menace*. *Ultimate Star Wars* refers to him as, "A child born of prophecy, possibly conceived by the will of the Force itself."[1] Thus, the prophecy of "the one who will bring balance to the Force" is revealed to the audience. Presumably, this messianic figure was to come from a fatherless conception. Throughout Anakin's training as a Jedi, the prudence of which was debated among the Jedi, his role as the potential "Chosen One" was frequently called into question. He was no Jesus figure in that he was prone to prideful and immature outbursts that teetered on violence, usually motivated by fear and anger. From his youth the dark side had an influence on him, especially fear and grief over the loss of loved ones, and Jedi such as Mace Windu admitted they did not trust him.

Nevertheless, he also demonstrated remarkable goodness as a child. He was hospitable to Qui-Gon and his party in order to protect them from a sand storm, and "He willingly commits to a dangerous activity that could easily injure or kill him in order to help complete strangers."[2] His generosity is impeccable, and his mother says of him, "He knows nothing of greed." How a good person could be turned into something so evil was a topic George Lucas intended to explore with Anakin's character.[3]

Knight Fall

Anakin's fall to the dark side, like the rest of us, did not happen overnight. He compromises his conscience slowly through a few significant events that lead him further from the "straight and narrow." First, he struggles greatly with authority, oftentimes taking it upon himself to do what he believes must be done to achieve his ends. This goes even to the point of disobedience, something that hints at Qui-Gon's style. However, it is the polar opposite of his master, Obi-Wan, who provides brilliant contrast to Anakin throughout the franchise. Anakin's success thanks to his giftedness only inflates his hubris. We see this throughout *Attack of the Clones* and *The Clone Wars*. While Anakin also shows a substantial amount of humility, concern for others, and virtue, he eventually forgoes these and embraces the darkness in his quest for greater power, namely to save Padme, and for galactic order and peace.

Second, Anakin's romantic interest in Padme and subsequent love affair represents how he lets his desires dictate his actions, as opposed to prudence and wisdom. As the *Catechism of the Catholic Church* teaches, "The alternative is clear: either man governs his passions and finds peace, or he lets himself be dominated by them and becomes unhappy."[4] Anakin is certainly passionate, and this was oftentimes used for the good in battle and for others, especially during *The Clone Wars*. However, he is unable to restrain it; his passion enflames to the point of intense desire and aggression. We see his lack of self-restraint in his relationship with Padme, for whom he has harbored affections since he was a child. His choice to reveal his desire for her and pursue something he has promised to forego as a Jedi is evidence of his lack of self-control and weakening character. Once they are secretly married and continue their relationship in the shadows, Anakin becomes accustomed to deception and is well beyond living fully in the light.

While Anakin's slip from Jedi ideals is prettied for the audience through his love for Padme, we see a darker side of his fall through his hate. The primary source of this is his final interaction with his mother on Tatooine in the hands of the Tusken Raiders. As Shmi dies in his arms in *Attack of the Clones*, Anakin's loss and inability to save her life boils over into absolute rage and the slaughter of Shmi's captors, including women and children. Again, the audience is offered an opportunity to engage in this moral slip with Anakin and sympathize with him. Such anger may seem excusable, but Anakin's continued struggle with his conscience—even years later, to the point of killing an unarmed Count Dooku in front of Palpatine at the beginning of *Revenge of the Sith*—demonstrates he is still aware of authentic good and evil.

Using the Force: *Star Wars* and Catholicism

Star Wars, though subtly, recognizes the Cardinal virtues of prudence, justice, fortitude, and temperance that Anakin should have demonstrated, as well as highlights the deadly sins of pride, lust, and wrath that he ought to have avoided. In each of these we see the exact opposite from Kenobi. [*The Clone Wars* SPOILERS follow in this paragraph.] Obi-Wan is always humble, restrained, and prudent. Obi-Wan also had a romantic attraction to Dutchess Satine Kryze in his youth and later when reunited with her during the Clone Wars; however, he remained resolute in his commitment to the Jedi even as he continued to love Satine with an authentic, self-sacrificing love. Furthermore, while Obi-Wan certainly experiences emotion, like sorrow, he does not give in to his hate and allow the dark side to get its foot in the door of his heart. In multiple instances we see human weakness growing to virtuous sainthood in Obi-Wan, while Anakin's human weakness falls gradually into the slavery of sin and darkness.

Caught in an intricate web forged by Darth Sidious, Anakin falls into a compromising situation in which he is full of doubt and fear. In choosing the apparent good of saving Padme's life, he betrays his Jedi brethren and becomes Darth Vader. McDowell notes, "Anakin does not by this time perceive the dark side as evil but rather (wrongly) as a different and better way of achieving his *good* purposes."[5] George Lucas's instruction to Hayden Christensen as he plays Anakin/Vader at this juncture is telling: "There's always good in you at this point. The good part is always saying 'What am I doing?' and the bad part is saying 'I'm doing this for Padme, I'm doing this for us, it'll be better for the universe, it'll be better for everybody.'"[6]

As we have seen, this turn to darkness was years in the making as Anakin broke rule after rule and compromised his conscience so completely that his loyalties came to a head and he was forced to choose between two supposed options. First, he could side with the Jedi (in whom he had recently lost confidence), the light side of the Force alone, and the potential loss of Padme in childbirth as he was foreseeing in his visions. Second, he could favor his friendship with Palpatine (who was a mentor and advisor), embrace the dark side's power and secrets in addition to his current light side powers, and pursue the potential to save Padme.

Interestingly, it is possible that Anakin's dreams about Padme's death in childbirth, which serve as a primary motivation for his turn to darkness, may have been perpetuated by Sidious himself. In the opera scene from *Revenge of the Sith* mentioned earlier, Sidious tells Anakin that Sidious's master, Darth Plagueis, was able to influence the midi-chlorians to create life, possibly hinting that Anakin's conception was caused by Plagueis. This is pure speculation, of course, yet Sidious tells us that Plagueis taught his apprentice all he knew. It is reasonable that Sidious would have been able to do something as menial as influence Anakin's dreams with visions of Padme dying, which would also explain how Sidious knew about Anakin's dreams and fears. Anakin then allowed this fear to overwhelm him, despite Yoda's advice to "Train yourself to let go of everything you fear to lose" (*Revenge of the Sith*). Palpatine capitalizes on Anakin's fear in order to sway Anakin's allegiance to himself.

Here we find another twist of circumstances, because the very thing Anakin wished to achieve by turning to the Sith, saving Padme from death, ended up being the probable cause of her death. The best explanation we receive for Padme's death is she "lost the will to live," and this can only be attributed to the fact that she has seen what Anakin has become, what he has done to the Jedi and the younglings at the Temple, and what he does to her on the landing platform on Mustafar. We ought to realize that whatever "good" we hope to achieve by allowing or even turning to evil, will only backfire on us as well as our loved ones.

We must remember Christ's promise, "I came so that they might have life and have it more abundantly" (Jn 10:10). Satan promises similar lies, but never delivers on them. In fact, the opposite proves true. As we give in to evil and compromise the truth, we become slaves to sin. This is displayed accurately with Anakin as Darth Vader. "He is more machine now than man, twisted and evil," remarks Obi-Wan of Vader in *Return of the Jedi*. McDowell reflects:

> His own humanity is destroyed in the turn to the dark side, as symbolized by these biotechnologies required for basic life-support, including the armorlike attire that masks from view both the human and his dehumanization; his great Jedi potential is never realized because of the extent of his injuries (he cannot use Force-Lightning due to his prosthetic arms, and he has roughly 80 percent of the Emperor's power when before his fall he had the potential to have 200 percent of it).[7]

Evil always falls short of its empty promises. Sin is never worth it, though usually we discover this truth too late. While Anakin's tragedy is fictional, we may distill poignant Christian truths from his experiences.

Savior & Redemption

As Darth Vader, Anakin became ruthless and merciless, constantly feeding off of his own pain and misery to fuel the power of the dark side for his purposes. Yet, light and hope remained for Anakin, as they always remain for us. Padme knew this, and her dying words to Kenobi were in recognition that there was still good in Anakin. This sentiment may have been passed on to Luke in the intense experience of his childbirth, because he echoes his mother's words often in *Return of the Jedi* as he recognizes the good remaining in Anakin, the conflict between light and dark still present in his heart.

Sidious was aware of this light as well, and we see much of Sidious testing his apprentice's resolve and loyalty throughout the novel *Lords of the Sith*. Even Sidious senses the good still in Vader, "The barest flicker of persistent light,"[8] he calls it. All throughout *Lords of the Sith* we see Sidious sensing Vader's thoughts to overthrow him. Vader himself tells Luke in *The Empire Strikes Back*, "You can destroy the Emperor, he has foreseen this." Luke becomes the beacon of light calling out to the residual "flicker of persistent light" of Anakin Skywalker buried deep in the recesses of Darth Vader.

Vader and Luke's confrontation before the Emperor on the Death Star is nothing short of epic. The degree of manipulation is layers deep at the Emperor's design, and the primary objective is to lure Luke into darkness. Hodge notices:

Luke undergoes a conversion—away from the violent, swashbuckling hero to the monk-like Jedi knight who gives up on violence and anger. At the climactic end of "Return of the Jedi," Luke refuses his chance to kill Vader—and indeed tries to save him—aware that by using violence he risks becoming a half-human enslaved to a false master, who promises liberation through anger and hate.[9]

At the most pivotal moment we see Luke, having returned the blow Vader dealt him by severing his hand, finally understanding the potential of following in his Father's footsteps. He sees they both share a mechanical limb, and perhaps Luke remembers the lesson from the cave on Dagobah—that evil lies not only without but also within. He chooses an unexpected path as Hodge recognizes:

> Redemptive violence and heroism are set aside for a spiritual path of nonviolent love... Crucially, the story here turns from Luke becoming a violent victor to a loving victim who is willing to give his life rather than take another's life. In suffering and confronting evil with love, evil can be transformed, resisted, and overcome.[10]

If restricted to viewing only the original trilogy, we come to the conclusion that Luke is a messianic Christ figure who saves his father from darkness, leads to the overthrow of the evil Sith Emperor, and restores the galaxy to goodness. All of these are true, as Anakin affirms in his final words. Following the defeat of the

Emperor, Luke is anxious to get Anakin off the collapsing Death Star. Anakin asks Luke to remove the Vader mask, symbolic of his conversion, though it will hasten his death. Anakin then tells Luke to leave him. Luke says, "No. You're coming with me. I'll not leave you here. I've got to save you," to which Anakin replies, "You already have, Luke." Anakin's dying words were, "You were right about me. Tell your sister, you were right."

We learn in the novel *Bloodline* that Luke indeed shared this experience with Leia. She, however, has a much more difficult time forgiving her father, because she writhed in pain in her cell on the Death Star at the age of nineteen as Vader tortured her mercilessly.[11] Leia discusses her feelings:

> "Sometimes I felt as if the only thing that kept me going in the aftermath of Alderaan was the strength of my hatred for Vader," for my father [she thinks to herself]. As always when Leia thought about this, she called upon what Luke had told her of their father's last hours. He had renounced darkness, saved Luke, and become Anakin Skywalker again. Whenever Luke told the story, a beatific smile lit up his face. His memories of that event gave him a level of comfort and even joy that sustained him. Those were memories Leia couldn't share.[12]

Later Leia thought about how she would explain her parentage to her son, Ben Solo. Her conclusion was to summarize: "Vader had in the end been redeemed. Anakin Skywalker had returned. The dark side had been defeated by the light."[13] Leia is able to come to this conclusion in her mind, but in her heart she could not forgive him. Thinking back on a conversation with Luke, she remembers:

> "He was Anakin Skywalker when he fell in love with our mother," Luke would say, taking her hand gently in his. "And he became Anakin Skywalker again in the last hour of his life. He came back from the dark side, Leia. They said it could never be done, but our father did it. He made the journey because of his love for us." Leia believed Luke. She could feel that truth within him, but it was difficult for her to find solace in this the way Luke did. How could Vader torture her without mercy if he had that good inside? He'd still had the power to make the right choice, but had instead forced her to suffer.[14]

As true as Luke's saving figure is, when we are exposed to the prequels, and the centrality of those six films hones in more closely on the tragedy and triumph of Anakin Skywalker, we see that he too fulfills the self-sacrificing messianic savior figure, thereby fulfilling his prophecy. Consequently, Anakin comes to fulfill what Obi-Wan said to him on the banks of the lava flow on Mustafar, "You were the Chosen One. It was said that you would destroy the Sith, not join them; bring balance to the Force, not leave it in darkness." This he did by overthrowing Palpatine and saving his son, Luke. Roy Anker illustrates the significance of this event, "Two completely unexpected and stunning acts of selfless bravery, one fast upon the other, defeat the vast metaphysical evil that is a hair's breadth from completely extinguishing the slowly dimming light of human kindness."[15] In addition Anker writes:

> At the cost of his own life, Vader acts to save his son, and in doing so...he is restored to full spiritual brotherhood with Obi-Wan and Yoda. In destroying the evil that first seduced him, Vader once again becomes a Jedi. ... Through the son's witness of love, the father is redeemed, and the father and son meet in reconciliation and true communion.[16]

This action involves conversion and grace with the result of Anakin being reunited with the *Star Wars* version of the Communion of Saints.

It seems both Luke and Anakin share the role as savior. Anakin was the one foretold in the prophecy, but he lost his path for a time. The Force used his son to bring him back so he could fulfill his destiny. The Force struck back, as Plagueis warned Sidious, and restored the light. By saving his father, Luke helped complete the prophecy and save the galaxy, and they both achieved this through self-sacrifice, like Christ.

To add another twist to the role of the prophecy [*Rebels* season 3 SPOILERS follow], when Obi-Wan finally kills Maul in battle on Tatooine, Maul realizes that Kenobi is protecting someone. Dying, Maul asks, "Is it the chosen one?," to which Kenobi responds, "He is." Maul's last words are, "He will avenge us." Maul's character could be summed up in that one word, revenge. What Maul sees as revenge, Obi-Wan would see as a righting of wrongs, an appropriate reordering of the galaxy, or a rebalancing of the Force. The biggest point for us here is that Obi-Wan identifies Luke as the

Chosen One, not Anakin. In the end, it will be both Anakin and Luke, father and son, who fulfill the prophecy together.

While Anakin needed Luke's participation in the grand scheme to fulfill the prophecy, Jesus did not need anyone's. Nevertheless, Christ wills to make us all partakers in his saving victory. He allowed Simon to help him carry his cross, he sent his Church out into the world to spread the Gospel, and he calls us to be his hands and feet in the world. While there are important differences, the fruits of salvation won both in *Star Wars* and in reality are shared by many.

---

[1] *Ultimate Star Wars* (New York: DK Penguin Random House, 2015), 38.

[2] Caleb Grimes, *Star Wars Jesus: A Spiritual Commentary on the Reality of the Force* (Enumclaw, WA: WinePress Publishing, 2007), 188.

[3] Bill Moyers, *The Mythology of Star Wars with George Lucas and Bill Moyers* (Public Affairs Television, Inc., 1999), https://vimeo.com/groups/183185/videos/38026023 (accessed 21 July 2017).

[4] *Catechism of the Catholic Church*, 2d ed. (Citta del Vaticano: Libreria Editrice Vaticana, 1997), § 2339.

[5] John C. McDowell, *The Gospel According to Star Wars: Faith, Hope, and the Force* (Louisville, Westminster John Knox Press, 2007), 80

[6] Ibid., 80-81.

[7] Ibid., 84.

[8] James Luceno, *Star Wars: Tarkin*, Audiobook narrated by Euan Morton (Random House Audio, 2014), approximately 3:44:00.

[9] Joel Hodge, "How 'Star Wars' Answers Our Biggest Religious Questions: The Movies Take on – and Subvert – Christian Themes," *The Washington Post* (21 April 2015) https://www.washingtonpost.com/posteverything/wp/2015/04/21/how-star-wars-answers-our-biggest-religious-questions/?utm_term=.4de7970e2ea0 (accessed 24 March 2017).

[10] Ibid.

[11] Claudia Gray, *Star Wars: Bloodline,* Audiobook narrated by January LaVoy (Random House Audio, 2016).

[12] Ibid., 4:32:13.

[13] Ibid., 4:35:46.

[14] Ibid., 9:32:43.

[15] Roy M. Anker, *Catching Light: Looking for God in the Movies* (Grand Rapids, MI: William B. Eerdmans Publishing Company, 2004), 220.

[16] Ibid., 236.

Chapter 8: Life, Death, and Afterlife

"An old friend has learned the path to immortality."
– Yoda (*Revenge of the Sith*)

Each character's life within the *Star Wars* saga is filled with choices, hundreds each day, just like us. Also like us they have the opportunity to do good or evil, to follow the light side of the Force or the dark. The concept of choice and free will is a strong underlying theme of the franchise. Anakin's entire character development spanning two trilogies, animated series, novels, and comic books is fraught with the ups and downs of the consequences resulting from his choices. We see him free and experiencing the joys of life as a Jedi, and we sense the depth of his fall into the slavery of the dark side as Darth Vader. The slavery to sin evident in the dark side may be why Mace Windu in *Revenge of the Sith* speaks of the "oppression of the Sith." The dark side is truly oppressive, and the Sith reflect this in their dealings with the galaxy, thereby oppressing it. These are clear warnings for us in reality. The choices we make determine our character and our path, yet there is always hope. Characters in *Star Wars* always have the opportunity to turn back to the light, and conversion to God is always an option for us.

Thy Will be Done

One aspect of the Force we have discussed briefly is its will. We noted in "Chapter 4: The Nature of the Force" that the Force is personal enough to have a will, not merely an Eastern spirituality type of impersonal force. In *Star Wars*, the Force has a plan, brings things about, even brings people together. In *The Phantom Menace*, Qui-Gon says of Anakin, "Finding him was the will of the Force, I have no doubt of that." In the Mortis arc of *The Clone Wars*, the Force-wielder known as the Father says, "I have done nothing. I am merely letting the will of the Force take shape." Throughout the novel *Lost Stars*, the two prominent characters, Thane Kyrell and Ciena Ree, are brought back together over and over again by events beyond coincidental, even though Thane refuses to believe in the Force until years of coincidences open him to some degree of faith.[1]

Even Sith recognize the operation of the will of the Force. In the novel *Tarkin*, Vader and Sidious are noticing events that seem an interesting coincidence revolving around the planet Murkhana. When asked about the possibility of coincidence by the Emperor, "Vader knew the reply, 'There are no coincidences, Master.' 'And *that*, my apprentice, is why Murkhana matters to us. Because the dark side of the Force has for whatever reason brought that world to our attention once more.'"[2] Sidious and Vader know there are no coincidences with the Force.

Similarly, in Catholicism we call God's plan providence, which is also without coincidence. We believe God has a plan and works in the lives of all to bring about his will, while allowing us to either participate with his will or to work against it. An essential element of living the Christian life is to seek God's will and live in conformity with it. The Blessed Virgin Mary possessed the special grace of being conceived without Original Sin, what we call the Immaculate Conception. During her life she also never committed any personal sins, because her will was completely in conformity with the will of God. In other words, she only ever wanted what God wanted. Jesus was unique in that he had both a human and divine will, yet there was no duplicity, because his human will was always in complete conformity with his Divine will.

What we find from the lives of those who live in conformity with God's will, namely the Saints, are lives of peace, knowledge, serenity, harmony, and God (veritably the five elements of the Jedi Code listed in the following section), even in the midst of great trials, suffering, death, and abandonment. Following the will of God brings good things, even in bad times, just as Jedi following the will of the Force find peace and serenity even during terrible experiences.

On the opposite side, those who are steeped in the dark side, like Vader, find themselves tormented, vexed, turbulent, and disheveled even during times of peace and prosperity. Opposing the light is really working against the will of the Force, just as opposing God's will is turning against God. The results of both courses are also clear. Evil promises all good things, yet it delivers only bad, while goodness promises resurrection (through the cross, of course) and delivers on its promise without fail. May we all seek to be saints and conform our wills to that of God.

For those who fail to follow God's will and give in to darkness, there is always hope. Yoda's instruction to Luke in *The Empire Strikes Back* would seem authoritatively pessimistic when he says, "If once you start down the dark path, forever will it dominate your destiny, consume you it will, as it did Obi-Wan's apprentice." At first consideration, it would seem there is no hope of conversion for those who dabble or fall completely into darkness. Then, at the end of *Return of the Jedi*, we see Vader's conversion and redemption. Therefore, we must understand Yoda's tutelage as general and not absolute. It must be possible for one to return from the dark side, and even Yoda has seen this during the Clone Wars era. Other than Anakin, both Asajj Ventress and Quinlan Vos went down very dark paths, yet came back to the light. All of these have been discussed in the earlier chapter on the Sith. Thus, Yoda must mean this in a loose sense.

The point for us to recognize here is conversion is always possible, even for someone as far gone as Vader, both in depth to the dark side and the amount of time spent in such corruption. Similarly, even the most hardened sinner, having spent decades in the service of evil, is capable of a full conversion and may be redeemed through God's grace. There is always the opportunity to turn back to God and his will, no matter how mired in sin someone may seem.

Death & Afterlife

Every religion must address what happens when we die. This question seems to be innate in the human mind, which turns to religion for an answer. The realm of *Star Wars* addresses this topic as well. In *Star Wars Aftermath: Empire's End*, Temmin "Snap" Wexley's father is buried on the planet Akiva. At the funeral, the following blessing is offered, which echoes the "ash to ash and dust to dust" of Christianity: "He may return to Akiva as a child of Akiva. From water they arise, to water they return. Atoms to atoms."[3] It is believed throughout the franchise that all people become one with the Force at death, probably because all life is linked to the Force. Yoda affirms, "Each life, a flame in the Force is."[4] This correlates with God's will that all people join him in heaven, because he loves us and we are made in his image and likeness; however, those who turn their backs to God through mortal sin merit eternal damnation.

Christians express belief in the afterlife in the Nicene and Apostles' Creeds, and the Jedi have one as well; it is called the Jedi Code: "There is no emotion, there is peace. There is no ignorance, there is knowledge. There is no passion, there is serenity. There is no chaos, there is harmony. There is no death, there is the Force."[5] The first time a *Star Wars* audience encountered the concept of death for the Jedi is between Obi-Wan and Darth Vader in *A New Hope*. As they are dueling Obi-Wan says, "You can't win, Darth. If you strike me down, I shall become more powerful than you can possibly imagine." This suggests an afterlife. When Vader kills Obi-Wan, his body disappears, and Obi-Wan almost immediately begins speaking to Luke through locutions (i.e., an audio-only apparition) and later in full visual apparitions. For instance, after Yoda dies in *The Empire Strikes Back*, Luke despairingly says, "I can't do it, Artoo. I can't go on alone." Luke then hears Obi-Wan's voice saying, "Yoda will always be with you." Luke looks up and sees Obi-Wan walking toward him through the swamp as a blue, shimmering spirit with whom Luke converses. This idea is well recognized in Catholicism with locutions, visions, and apparitions, usually involving Christ, Mary, Saints, or Angels.

At Yoda's death we see the same thing happen; his body disappears as his blanket gently settles to the bed. As far as we knew in 1980 this is the way all Jedi pass away — a unique feature of death for them not shared by other sentient beings like Stormtroopers or rebels who simply fall to the ground. We are not surprised to see Anakin fail to fade away at the end of *Return of the Jedi*, probably due to him being in his suit as Vader. Nonetheless, he appears as his former Jedi self at the end of the film. If he was granted this kind of afterlife with Obi-Wan and Yoda, why did he not fade away at death as well?

When the prequel films were released, the *Star Wars* audience learned even more about dying and the Force. At the end of *The Phantom Menace*, Qui-Gon Jinn dies in battle. Unlike Obi-Wan and Yoda, he simply falls to the ground and his body is later burned, as Luke burned Anakin's on the Endor forest moon. We come to understand that this is the normal death for Jedi, like everyone else, and that Obi-Wan and Yoda's experiences are the unique ones.

At Qui-Gon's funeral Obi-Wan looks to his new padawan, Anakin, and says, "He is one with the Force, Anakin. You must let go" (*The Phantom Menace*). This seems to be a reference to the Hindu teaching that one may be released from the cycle of reincarnation at death, what they call moksha, and become one with the universal force, Brahman. Similarly, Buddhists seek to end the cycle of reincarnation and achieve what they call nirvana.

When Jedi return as Obi-Wan did, they are known as Force ghosts. George Lucas may very well have been inspired by the idea of Buddhist bodhisattvas, who forego entering Nirvana to help others attain this goal. Hodge tells us, "Lucas came to describe himself as a 'Buddhist Methodist,'" having grown up Methodist to some degree and espousing some Buddhist ideas later in life.[6] Lucas admitted in an interview many of his conclusions in life may be found in his films, so we should not be surprised at this.[7] However, unlike Catholic Saints or angels who appear in apparitions like a Force ghost, bodhisattvas are reincarnated into another human life. What occurs in *Star Wars* films relates to the Saints of Catholicism as well as to Eastern ideas, but it does not correlate perfectly to either. We may suggest, though, that it is much closer to Catholicism than an Eastern release from the cycle of reincarnation, as there is no hint of reincarnation in the franchise.

Immortality

In *Revenge of the Sith*, fans learn still more about death in the Force. The Jedi seem to have previously thought that when they died they simply became one with the Force, and their independent personalities ceased to exist, just like everyone else in the galaxy. What Lucas develops further in *Revenge of the Sith* is a thought again more Christian than Eastern. This is where the Jedi first learn of being able to defy oblivion and maintain their conscious self after physical death. We receive more of a teaser than anything when Yoda tells Obi-Wan he has further training for him during his exile on Tatooine at the end of the film. Yoda reveals that Qui-Gon Jinn has returned from the netherworld of the Force. *Ultimate Star Wars* explains, "By the will of the Force, Qui-Gon's spirit survives, and Yoda eventually hears Qui-Gon's disembodied voice."[8] Yoda will need to teach Obi-Wan how to commune with him to learn this immortal ability for himself.

Just watching the films, we are forced to read between the lines to understand this is how Obi-Wan and Yoda learn to appear as Force ghosts later and why their deaths are unique. *Ultimate Star Wars* confirms, "After Order 66, Yoda informs Obi-Wan that Qui-Gon's spirit lives, and that he will resume communication with Obi-Wan, teaching him to become one with the Force."[9] A Jedi who becomes a Force ghost has some resemblance to the resurrected Jesus or apparitions of Saints. In the Apostles' Creed Christians profess believing in "the resurrection of the body, and life everlasting." Lucas was clearly influenced by aspects of Christian thought throughout his masterpiece.

During the "Lost Missions" (what would have been season 6) of *The Clone Wars*, we delve most profoundly into the mystery of immortality. [SPOILERS through the rest of this section.] We follow Yoda through his trials before his training for immortality, which take us deeper into his experience with Qui-Gon prior to *Revenge of the Sith*, and ultimately how and why he was allowed to achieve immortality. As *Ultimate Star Wars* notes, "Yoda knows more about the nature of the Force than almost any Jedi Knight, but his experiences on a mysterious planet teach him the astonishing secret of immortality."[10]

Over some time, and with considerable doubt about the authenticity of the locutions, Yoda becomes convinced Qui-Gon is reaching out to him from the netherworld of the Force. *Ultimate Star Wars* continues, "Guided by the spirit of Qui-Gon Jinn, who speaks of a way to retain one's consciousness after death, Yoda journeys to a strange world near the center of the galaxy. He finds a place rich in the Force. ... Five Force Priestesses intercept him."[11] These priestesses are all "one ancient being" who died long ago; "she is conscious in the Force and she has a limited ability to manifest," which is why Yoda and Obi-Wan can learn to be immortal, because "It's been done before."[12]

Before testing him and beginning his training to find immortality, they ask him, "Do you come to us with only good intention and light in your heart?" We may surmise this great gift of immortality is something only available to those who are aligned with the light. "Yoda learns that...he will need to pass their trials to gain the knowledge that Qui-Gon spoke of."[13] By way of introduction, one of the Priestesses explains, "At death, in order for you to preserve your identity, you must know yourself, your true self, and then let go." This seems quite Buddhist on the surface; however, the context becomes clear in the first test.

Launching into the tests, we see more wisdom and the recurrence of strong themes in *Star Wars*. First, Yoda must recognize the potential evil that resides within himself and rebuke it, letting it go, thus choosing to follow the will of the Force and grow in goodness and holiness as he has been doing throughout his life. This is my favorite of the tests, because it relates most strongly to growing in Christian holiness and virtue. In a fight with his evil self who says, "Yoda plays not with me anymore," Yoda continues to deny knowing his foe and is beaten badly. The tide only turns when Yoda recognizes his enemy within and defeats it: "Recognize you, I do. Part of me you are, yes. Power over me, you have not. Through patience and training, it is I who control you. Control over me you have not. My dark side you are; reject you I do." At that, the evil manifestation of Yoda disintegrates like ash in the wind.

Once he succeeds, a Priestess says, "You have conquered your hubris, now face the temptations you must." As the second test, he experiences a pleasant but false vision which he must reject, despite its allure over reality, and embrace the truth as it is. For the third test Yoda engages in a unique conflict with powers of the dark side and prevails. In the final scenario he declares, "Tempted I will not be. Sacrifice all, I am ready to do." In saintly fashion, Yoda completely abandons himself for the good, even to the point of martyrdom, just as Christ sacrificed himself for us all. After this he will be ready to receive the knowledge and begin training for immortality.

At one point in Yoda's trials, he empties himself of his will, saying, "Let the Force guide, I will." What a profound statement we may make about God. The next time we are experiencing a trial, we might calm ourselves and say, "Let the Lord guide, I will." Like Yoda, the will of God is leading us to immortality in heaven. In order to achieve this, we must abandon our wills and embrace the will of God for our lives, just as a Jedi follows the will of the Force. Furthermore, it requires that we renounce evil, including the evil inside ourselves, which Yoda demonstrates, in order to grow in holiness.

Ghost Anakin

A common question of discerning fans is why was Anakin transformed into a Force ghost if Obi-Wan and Yoda had to undergo such special training? [*The Clone Wars* SPOILERS follow in the next two paragraphs.] In a special Q&A session about *The Clone Wars*, supervising director Dave Filoni, who worked as number two to George Lucas on the series, was asked this question. Filoni responds that what we see in the programs are Yoda's trials, not the training, "to see if he is even worthy of this knowledge and would he abuse the knowledge and somewhat pervert the power."[14] This further illustrates that the light is the original nature of the Force. Darkness is a perversion of the light, not the true nature of the Force, nor how people are to relate to it. Filoni continues, "He still has to learn this process from Qui-Gon, which is why he tells Obi-Wan he is communicating with Qui-Gon."[15] In typical Dave Filoni style, he refuses to answer the question directly, because he wants fans to enjoy speculation.

Filoni does, however, offer the hint that they included a scene in these episodes where Yoda asks Anakin if he really spoke to Qui-Gon on Mortis during the Clone Wars. Anakin says he thinks he did, but Anakin also reports that Obi-Wan is skeptical.[16] At that point the host of the panel, Leland Chee, says, "Because Yoda is talking to Anakin, it's almost like he's planting the seed in Anakin's mind."[17] At that moment, Filoni, responds, "OH!," while pointing to Leland, and looking at the audience says, "Yes, Leland. Darn, you've figured it out."[18] This is one reason why Filoni earlier stated he appreciates how George Lucas changed the Force ghost of Anakin in the Special Edition version of *Return of the Jedi* to the Hayden Christensen portrayal rather than the original Sebastian Shaw, because it is the image of Anakin at the "last moment that he was the good person. ... It doesn't make sense, mythologically, for him to maintain the guise of the old man afterward in the Force, because he was never good."[19] Filoni continues, "He was never balanced when he was that person. He was the wicked old man, so he has to shed that skin like everything else."[20]

As Catholics we have the hope and the opportunity to experience the bliss of heaven thanks to the salvation won by Jesus through his Paschal Mystery. While this does not require special training, *per se*, those of us who lead the Christian lifestyle are engaged in a training process like Jedi. Like Anakin, though, we may also convert near the moment of death and enjoy the everlasting beatitude of heaven.

---

[1] Claudia Gray, *Star Wars: Lost Stars*, Audiobook narrated by Pierce Cravens (Random House Audio, 2015).

[2] "*Star Wars: Tarkin* – Exclusive Excerpt!" http://www.starwars.com/news/star-wars-tarkin-exclusive-excerpt (accessed 7-7-17).

[3] Chuck Wendig, *Star Wars Aftermath: Empire's End*, Audiobook narrated by Marc Thompson (Random House Audio, 2017), 15:16:40.

[4] Christie Golden, *Star Wars: Dark Disciple,* Audiobook narrated by Marc Thompson (Random House Audio, 2015), 21:25.

[5] Ibid., 8:58:40.

[6] Joel Hodge, "How 'Star Wars' Answers Our Biggest Religious Questions: The Movies Take on – and Subvert – Christian Themes," *The Washington Post* (21 April 2015) https://www.washingtonpost.com/posteverything/wp/2015/04/21/how-star-wars-answers-our-biggest-religious-questions/?utm_term=.4de7970e2ea0 (accessed 24 March 2017). John C. McDowell, *The Gospel According to Star Wars: Faith, Hope, and the Force* (Louisville, Westminster John Knox Press, 2007), 20.

[7] Bill Moyers, *The Mythology of Star Wars with George Lucas and Bill Moyers* (Public Affairs Television, Inc., 1999), https://vimeo.com/groups/183185/videos/38026023 (accessed 21 July 2017).

[8] *Ultimate Star Wars* (New York: DK Penguin Random House, 2015), 22.

[9] Ibid.

[10] Ibid., 72.

[11] Ibid.

[12] "Force Priestesses – The Lost Missions Q&A, Star Wars: The Clone Wars," Star Wars Youtube Channel (published 26 November 2014) https://www.youtube.com/watch?v=iKWDZaxUoMg (accessed 26 July 2017).

[13] *Ultimate Star Wars*, 72.

[14] "Force Ghosts – The Lost Missions Q&A, Star Wars: The Clone Wars," Star Wars Youtube Channel (published 4 December 2014) https://www.youtube.com/watch?v=iKWDZaxUoMg (accessed 26 July 2017).

[15] Ibid.

[16] Ibid.

[17] Ibid.

[18] Ibid.

[19] Ibid.

[20] Ibid.

Chapter 9: Further Commonalities

"The Force will be with you, always."
– Obi-Wan Kenobi (*A New Hope*)

Many additional connections between *Star Wars* and Catholicism are worthy of consideration. Several of these make great talking points with fans about *Star Wars*, because they are simpler connections that do not require lengthy explanation. This chapter will consider several such similarities.

May the Force be with You

For starters, the phrase, "May the Force be with you," resembles "May the Lord be with you," or "Peace be with you," as Catholics share at Mass. This also hearkens back to the centuries old English phrase at departure, "God be with ye," which was contracted to our present word, "goodbye." Christians have consistently wished the presence of God upon those they are greeting, praying amidst, or from whom they are departing. *Star Wars* hijacks such religious phraseology and inserts the Force in God's place.

The Force will be with You, Always

At the end of *A New Hope*, Obi-Wan's locution tells Luke, "Remember, the Force will be with you, always." This relates to the final words of Matthew's Gospel in which Jesus tells his apostles, "I am with you always, until the end of the age" (Mt 28:20). We also have the promise of the advocate, the Holy Spirit, to be with us always (Jn 14:16). At a time of completion and departure, both phrases offer comfort to those who must go on without their master's tutelage, at least temporarily. In Luke's case, he goes years without hearing from Obi-Wan again and even begins to wonder if the voice he heard from Obi-Wan during the trench run on the Death Star was in his head.[1] In time, with deeper training, Luke would come to better understand this presence ever with him. Often we also need training in prayer to hear the voice of God and discern his will for our lives. Sometimes we may go for years seemingly without hearing from God.

I Find Your Lack of Faith Disturbing

George Lucas included a dichotomy between secularization and faith as a theme in *Star Wars*. One of the first and most powerful examples of this is the conference room scene on the Death Star in *A New Hope*.

Using the Force: *Star Wars* and Catholicism

Admiral Motti contends, "This station is now the ultimate power in the universe. I suggest we use it," to which Darth Vader replies, "Don't be too proud of this technological terror you've constructed. The ability to destroy a planet is insignificant next to the power of the Force." Mockingly, Motti begins, "Don't try to frighten us with your sorcerer's ways, Lord Vader. Your sad devotion to that ancient religion has not helped you conjure up the stolen data tapes, or given you clairvoyance enough to find the Rebels' hidden fort…" Motti, choking, clutches his collar as Vader, a distance away, strangles him through the Force with one gloved hand raised in a pinching motion. Vader retorts, "I find your lack of faith disturbing." Commenting on this scene, John C. McDowell observes, "The secularist condescendingly rejects religion, but Vader's reaction of choking Motti by the mere power of his thought indicates that *Star Wars*'s sympathies are not with the secularist. It is Motti, not Vader, who plays the fool."[2]

Motti is hardly the minority, though; doubt reigns across the galaxy. When Luke first learns to use the Force on the Millennium Falcon in *A New Hope*, Han Solo expresses doubt. "Hokey religions and ancient weapons are no match for a good blaster at your side," he says. Luke ventures the reply, "You don't believe in the Force, do you?" Cynically, Han retorts:

> Kid, I've flown from one side of this galaxy to the other and I've seen a lot of strange stuff, but I've never seen anything to make me believe there's one all-powerful Force controlling everything. There's no mystical energy field that controls *my* destiny. It's all a lot of simple tricks and nonsense. (*A New Hope*)

Luke has his own hesitations about belief. Anker writes, "It will take virtually the entire saga for Luke Skywalker to fully trust the reality of the Force, in other words, to arrive at faith in something he cannot detect with his senses."[3]

Obi-Wan begins to show Luke how to use the Force by having him block non-lethal laser blasts from a training remote with his eyes covered. Obi-Wan instructs Luke saying, "Let go of your conscious self and act on instinct. … Your eyes can deceive you. Don't trust them. Stretch out with your feelings." Staub reminds us of King Solomon's words, "Trust in the Lord with all your heart, and do not rely on your own insight."[4] When Luke is successful, the skeptical Han Solo says, "I call it luck," to which Kenobi responds, "In my experience, there's no such thing as luck." Obi-Wan seems to grasp the concept of divine providence, which leaves nothing to chance and sees God's hand active in creation. He encourages Luke by saying, "That's good. You've taken your first step into a larger world."

Han Solo's doubt about the Force in *A New Hope* softens by the time Luke leaves to attack the Death Star. Han goes so far as to say, "May the Force be with you." This may be only placating Luke, but in time Han would change his mind about the Force. Over three decades later in Han's life, by the time we encounter him in *The Force Awakens*, he is talking to Rey and Finn about the Force. Rey questions, "The Jedi were real!?," to which Han replies, "I used to wonder about that myself. Thought it was just a bunch of mumbo-jumbo. A magical power holding together good and evil, the dark side and the light. Crazy thing is, it's true. The Force, the Jedi, all of it. It's all true." For some of us, faith is a gift that comes more easily, as it did for Luke.

For others, we natural skeptics and doubting Thomas disciples, it takes more time and evidence, as it did for Han.

Perhaps the most obvious lesson on the necessity of faith occurs during Luke's training on Dagobah in *The Empire Strikes Back*. When Luke's X-wing fighter sinks into the swamp, he seems to lose hope it can ever be freed. Yoda, irritated, says, "Always with you it cannot be done. Hear you nothing that I say?" Luke replies there is a big difference between moving stones and moving ships. Yoda sternly objects, "No! No different! Only different in your mind. You must unlearn what you have learned." Luke says, "All right, I'll give it a try," but Yoda rebukes him, "No! Try not. Do. Or do not. There is no try."

Master Yoda is trying to make this simple point clear: a Jedi who uses the Force must be full of faith and without doubt. Then, only then, will a Jedi work great feats through the Force. I am reminded of when the disciples approached Jesus after unsuccessfully trying to drive out a demon. They asked Jesus why they were unsuccessful, and he replied, "Because of your little faith. Amen, I say to you, if you have faith the size of a mustard seed, you will say to this mountain, 'Move from here to there,' and it will move. Nothing will be impossible for you" (Mt 17:20).

There is another strong biblical parallel to this lesson learned on Dagobah. In Matthew 14:22-33, Jesus walks on the water out to the disciples in their boat. On seeing Jesus, Peter asked Jesus to command him to come to Jesus on the water, to which Jesus acquiesced. Peter left the boat and walked on the water toward Jesus; however, Peter became scared, entertained doubts, and began to sink. Jesus caught Peter and said, "O you of little faith, why did you doubt?"

After the previous instruction about having faith, Luke attempts to lift the fighter from the swamp. It seems as if he might almost be able to do it, but he doubts and it sinks even deeper, much akin to Peter. He says to Yoda, "You want the impossible," and walks away. Yoda then proceeds to reach out with the Force to lift the huge fighter from the swamp, through the air, and sets it down gently on dry land. Luke is astonished and says to Yoda with wide eyes, "I don't, I don't believe it!" Yoda solemnly answers, "That is why you fail."

In "Chapter 3: What the Force is Not," we explored some aspects of the Force as a mystery. There we recognized that while mysteries cannot be fully understood, we may walk away from them with some insight, both negative realizations as well as positive information. Here, in our discussion of faith, we must recognize the side of the mystery we cannot understand. In our relationship with God, he will always exist beyond us in a degree of transcendence. This transcendence is held in tension with authentic immanence, but we must recognize our God is beyond us, and we are incapable of fully comprehending his majesty. This is a lesson those in the *Star Wars* galaxy must also learn about the Force. In both cases, faith becomes a form of trust in the divine—a belief in its existence and its working in creation, even though much of it is beyond our detection.

To have faith in the Force or in God does not mean one may not have evidence and experience to support such faith. It does not mean that one does not doubt. It is, rather, to be open and to participate in a relationship with God (in reality) or the Force (in *Star Wars* fantasy). In both cases we find it is we who change, who are brought to a new level of understanding and existence. For the Jedi, the highest level achieved is becoming one with the Force after death, yet retaining individual consciousness and the ability to interact with the galaxy. This is the *Star Wars* version of immortality. For the Christian, the highest level achieved is eternal life in heaven.

Intercessory Prayer

Prayer is also shared territory. In one scene of *The Empire Strikes Back*, Luke finds himself beaten and helpless, hanging beneath the Cloud City of Bespin. Consequently, he cries out in what seems like a prayer to the deceased Obi-Wan. This resembles praying to Saints. Luke cries out, "Ben! Ben, please!" He then turns to another source of aid, Leia Organa. He calls, "Hear me. Leia!" Through the possible intercession of Obi-Wan, and definitely through the Force, Leia senses Luke is in danger and needs her help. She instructs the crew of her ship to return to Cloud City where she finds Luke in peril. This is a fantastic parallel to prayer and intercession through the power of God.

As Catholics we see Saints interceding on our behalf. For example, the normal process to become a Saint requires two miracles worked through his or her intercession, one before beatification and the other following beatification and preceding canonization. Considering the remarkable number of Saints canonized in the last century; we have ample opportunity to research and explore the numerous documented and approved times Saints have interceded to provide God's help here on Earth and the recent miracles attributed to their intercession.

Communion of Saints

These examples of prayer and intercession further illustrate for us the Communion of Saints, the "cloud of witnesses" from Hebrews 12:1. The Communion of Saints refers to the unity of the Church as it exists in three different states of being: all of us who are part of the pilgrim Church working out our salvation here on earth, the suffering souls being purified in purgatory, and the triumphant souls who have been granted eternal bliss in heaven. United in Christ, we are one family, and we are capable of crossing those barriers in communication and aid, by the grace of God. In *Star Wars*, the Force also allows souls separated by space and even death to continue communicating with and helping one another.

Catholicism appreciates not only an individual person's relationship with God but also recognizes the importance of the community in relationship with God and each other. Many Christians today overemphasize one's "personal relationship with Christ." Such a relationship is essential; however, God's goal following the fall of humankind into Original Sin was the reunification of all as his people—the reuniting of all fallen humanity with one another in love.

Sin damages our good relationship with God, self, and others. Consequently, God's response has always been to repair each of those relationships. He wishes to repair our relationships with each other communally and our relationship with him as his people; this is what salvation history is all about. He began with Israel in the Old Testament and has worked all the way to the Church Christ founded in the New Testament—the Catholic Church—to bring his people together and unite them to himself.

How does this apply to *Star Wars*? In popular American storytelling there is often one main good guy who fights the bad guys, basically singlehandedly (John Wayne style). From the beginning George Lucas infused *Star Wars* with a teamwork and communal essence in contrast to rugged individualism. Consider *A New Hope*, for instance. Luke is the protagonist, but it takes a whole team of gifted yet insufficient individuals to pull off victory—together. This is not only a better reflection of reality, it is also more sound theologically. Luke needs the help of Obi-Wan to teach him about the Force and to use it to destroy the Death Star; Obi-Wan is too old to go about this business by himself and thereby needs the rest of the young team; Han is indebted to Jabba the Hutt, yet becomes entangled in this web of teamwork, even though he represents the Western swashbuckler motif; and Leia is the unconventional, no-nonsense damsel in distress.

Specifically considering Han Solo, Russell Dalton comments:

> Han Solo was not convinced by fancy speeches or sermons about the cause of the Rebellion or the Force. They actually seemed to make him all the more skeptical. But by being around people with a belief in something beyond themselves, people who are willing to die for a cause, Han is changed. He becomes a part of the community and starts to share the values and beliefs of the group.[5]

This reminds me of a catechetical quip, "The faith is not taught but caught." Actions speak louder than words, and being part of a community builds up all members as God intends.

The interconnectedness continues well beyond these four characters, especially as the films expand in number, yet it is clear that *Star Wars* values communal success above individual achievement. This is also a strongly Catholic ideal. Anker notes this theme speaking of the Ewoks in *Return of the Jedi*:

> The cute and furry little beasts, an unlikely source of any help, prove as game and vital in defeating the Empire as Han Solo and his machismo, Wookies, droids, Ewoks, crooks, princesses, con men, orphans, and priests—all join up to smite the foul and unholy Empire.[6]

Dalton further recognizes:

> George Lucas's filmmaking style highlights this communal motif. The climaxes of many of the *Star Wars* films cut back and forth between several scenes as the battles are fought on many fronts. As a result, the viewer is presented with the image of many people working together and coordinating their efforts in order to achieve a victory.[7]

The value placed on community may be best exemplified among the Jedi Order, who are somewhat a reflection of the Church. Timothy Paul Jones notes:

> To become a Jedi is to be committed to a community. ... Within this community, every

Jedi needs guidance and no Jedi stands alone. ... Not only do the Jedi draw wisdom from living mentors, but they also absorb the teachings of past masters. At the height of the Jedi Order, the Jedi Archives enshrine the ancient masters' insights in millions of holocrons, so that present and future Jedi can share their wisdom.[8]

The Church offers a similar handing on of wisdom with its spiritual and theological masters of the past, such as the Doctors of the Church. Like the Jedi, the Church's mission is to unite us together with one another and with God, as much as possible in this life, and ultimately in heaven for eternity.

Self-Sacrifice

Star Wars employs a strong theme of self-sacrifice on the part of heroes, which resonates strongly with audiences and reflects the self-sacrificing love of Christ. Jesus taught, "No one has greater love than this, to lay down one's life for one's friends" (Jn 15:13), which is a consistent theme in the franchise. The ultimate example of this is Luke's decision to lay down his life rather than kill his father and the resulting self-sacrifice of Anakin overthrowing the Emperor and Sith domination in *Return of the Jedi*. This is the epic conclusion to which the original and prequel trilogies are directed.

There are several more examples of self-sacrifice, though. Luke prefigures his decision in *Return of the Jedi*, committing unequivocally to what is right when he falls into oblivion rather than join Vader at the climax of *The Empire Strikes Back*. In *A New Hope*, Obi-Wan offers himself as a diversion to allow the others to escape, and—perhaps more importantly—distracts Vader from sensing that the farm boy running around the Death Star is his son. Rather than fight for his life on Cloud City, thereby putting his friends at risk, Han Solo takes a martyr's role by allowing himself to be frozen. Self-sacrifice eventually costs Han his life as he abandons his safety entirely in an effort to win back his fallen son, Ben, on the catwalk of Starkiller Base in *The Force Awakens*. This is one rare instance in which self-sacrifice appears unsuccessful, though it does cause turmoil in Kylo Ren.

Over time, as we are exposed to more Jedi and other heroes in the prequels, *The Clone Wars*, and *Rebels*, we see instances of self-sacrifice for the good of the community time and again. In recent films we have seen Chirrut Îmwe's "faith walk" in *Rogue One*, which is both a great example of self-sacrifice and faith in the Force. Luke finally offered himself completely through his self-manifestation projected on Crait to distract the First Order and allow the decimated remnants of the Resistance to escape, which leads to the dramatic climax of *The Last Jedi*. Similarly, the concluding episodes of Rebels [SPOILER] also witnesses the heroism of Kanan Jarrus in order to save his friends in what has become typical Jedi self-sacrifice. Such examples remind us, "Whoever finds his life will lose it, and whoever loses his life for my sake will find it" (Mt 10:39), especially for those who become Force ghosts.

Diversity and Inclusivity

Inclusivity is another theme worth noting. Consider the ethnocentric Empire of the original trilogy. It is nearly all white males in straight-laced, sterile, and technologically saturated environments. In stark contrast, we have the diversified rebellion consisting of a number of other species, though, admittedly only a few females in the original trilogy. While there is only one other human race than white in the original trilogy, the diversity improves over time. Rebel clothes and environments also tend to be more organic and natural than technologically cold.

The prequels included even more genders and races, and the franchise under Disney seems to be diversifying all the more. The point is the "bad guys" are always less diversified and inclusive, while the "good guys" are a collection of many more species and races. The word "catholic" means universal, and the Church is open to everyone, as God's plan of salvation with Christ opened beyond the Jewish community to all Gentiles. *Star Wars* reflects this. The Jedi Council is a great example of diversity and inclusivity with "beings of all races, shapes, sizes, and colors serving on the Jedi Council. ... The Council is a wise and respectable group of diverse individuals who work together and respect one another."[9] This has strong resemblance to the Church, exemplified by the college of bishops and cardinals.

Respect for Nature

Like Catholicism, *Star Wars* values a respect for nature. The living Force, after all, is bred by living things, so all life is sacred. We see the Empire and First Order in white, black, and gray, as well as on modern-looking ships, while the Jedi, Rebellion, and Resistance often don earthy tones, are pictured in natural landscapes, and frequent vegetative locations.

Conversely, the Empire was even willing to tear apart entire planets to harvest resources. Some such planets, known as "Legacy Worlds," are supposed to be preserved and protected by the government, like our national parks. In the *Ahsoka* novel, for example, she sees them tearing apart the planet Ilum to harvest kyber crystals to power the first Death Star they are building. The good guys use technology, but in better conformity with nature.

Overcoming Fear

An important sub-theme of the franchise is overcoming, or at least not giving in to, fear. This is also a strong theme in Christianity. Jones comments, "By focusing on forsaking one's fears, the *Star Wars* saga echoes a central theme of faith in Jesus. 'Do not be afraid,' the Lord commands nearly seventy times in the Scriptures."[10] This was also a central theme of Pope St. John Paul II's pontificate, as he repeated it constantly. According to Dave Filoni, this was something George Lucas espoused in his professional life. Distilling the core message he learned from Lucas in nearly one decade of producing *The Clone Wars*, Dave Filoni states, "It's just a true thing in life, as you've always said [George], just don't be afraid—to make no decision out of fear, that's key."[11]

As a Christian pastor, Timothy Paul Jones says he is convinced that "Fear arises when we realize that we are not in control. And, deep inside, each of us longs to be in control. That was the problem Anakin Skywalker faced," both with his mother's death and his dreams about Padme's death.[12] An antidote to fear is trust in the providence and will of God, or trust in the Force for the

Using the Force: *Star Wars* and Catholicism

Jedi. In one of the first scenes with Chirrut Îmwe in *Rogue One* on Jedha, he walks out among the Stormtroopers detaining Jyn Erso and Cassian Andor stating, "The Force is with me, and I am with the Force. And I fear nothing, for all is as the Force wills it." He overcomes his fear through absolute trust in the Force and submits himself to its will. Christians can learn from this example.

Recognizing Anakin's attachment and desire for control, Yoda assigned Anakin a padawan in *The Clone Wars*. Yoda hoped Anakin would learn to detach from people close to him more easily by watching Ahsoka Tano mature and became a Jedi Knight herself. This backfired somewhat, because the way Anakin and Ahsoka parted company may have further exacerbated Anakin's feelings of impotence and his desire for control. In *Revenge of the Sith*, Yoda counsels Anakin, "The fear of loss is a path to the dark side. … Train yourself to let go of everything you fear to lose."

Similarly, Jesus emphasizes the attitude we must have toward people and our possessiveness of them: "If any one comes to me without hating his father and mother, wife and children, brothers and sisters, and even his own life, he cannot be my disciple" (Lk 14:26). Jones interprets this scripture:

> [It requires] you to let go of the delusion that anything you call your own—whether people or properties, possessions or plans—actually belongs to you. It means recognizing everything in your life as the property of a power greater than your own. It means letting go of your lust for control.[13]

Letting go and trusting God helps to mitigate fear as well as leading to holiness.

Temptation

Temptation is a recurring theme in *Star Wars*, because Lucas is interested in the idea of choice determining our destiny. Characters in the franchise often realize at the most pivotal moments they have a choice to pursue the good or to turn to the easy path of evil. Jesus warns, "The gate is wide and the road broad that leads to destruction, and those who enter through it are many. How narrow the gate and constricted the road that leads to life. And those who find it are few" (Mt 7:13-14).

One of the most powerful moments of temptation in *Star Wars* is Darth Vader's temptation for Luke to join him after cutting off his hand in their duel on the Cloud City of Bespin in *The Empire Strikes Back*. Henderson explains:

> Vader first appeals to Luke's self-preservation instinct: "Don't make me destroy you." Then he attempts to lure Luke with...flattery and egoism: "You do not yet realize your importance. You have only begun to discover your power. Join me and I will complete your training." But neither of these can bring Luke to his side. Next Vader throws out a hook aimed at Luke's very hero values: "With our combined strength, we can end this destructive conflict and bring order to the galaxy."[14]

This last temptation was among the few to successfully seduce Anakin, as Sidious used the promise of peace in the galaxy to sway Anakin to his allegiance. This three-part temptation sequence echoes Christ's triple temptation by Satan in the desert before beginning his public ministry (see Mt 4: 1-11 and Lk 4: 1-13).

Corruption

Star Wars is clear in demonstrating that corruption is not only from without but also from within. McDowell affirms:

> In the prequels we are distinctly forced to see that the Empire is not an alien order, an invading force that conquers the "good" Republic by pure self-assertion. Instead, it is a cancerous growth within the Republic's own body, gaining its life by drawing on the tiredness, complacency, vice, and corruption that plague the Senate.[15]

This is a pertinent warning for us individually, as a Church, and as a society. We must not deny that the Jedi, as well as high-ranking members of the Catholic Church, are capable of corruption. The franchise includes examples of Jedi defectors like Count Dooku and Pong Krell. On a larger scale, during the Republic the Jedi "are extremely dominant and prolific. There is a Jedi academy and a huge organization that supports it, including the incredible Jedi library."[16] Grimes suggests, "In the midst of this wealth of power, the Jedi Council becomes comfortable, maybe even proud, and this leads to their decline."[17] We must be on the watch in our own spiritual lives to prevent the downfall experienced by the Jedi, both institutionally and personally. [SPOILERS through the end of this section.]

It seems the fall of the Jedi Order and their inability to see the machinations of the Sith at work is at least partially due to their own negligence and misdirected focus. Referring to padawan Ahsoka Tano's abandonment by the Jedi in *The Clone Wars* season 5 four-part finale, *Ultimate Star Wars* notes, "Ahsoka's expulsion and trial shake her beliefs to their core, giving her a clearer understanding of the ways the Jedi Order has compromised its duty to the Force by serving the political needs of the Galactic Republic."[18] Similarly, McDowell notes, "Even the Jedi Council, with its initial war support, its blindness to the Sith in its midst, and the way it treated Anakin, is similarly complicit in its own destruction."[19]

The moral compromising the Jedi fell into is a major theme of the novel *Dark Disciple* and indicates the level to which they were deteriorating before they were slaughtered in the Jedi Purge. The premise of the novel is that Count Dooku needs to be stopped for the sake of saving lives and ending the war. The Jedi wrestle with the moral maxim held by the Catholic Church, among others: "The end does not justify the means."[20] Mace Windu is the first to suggest that the Jedi assassinate Dooku, a thought Obi-Wan finds appalling and Sith-like. Mace defends his proposal, stating he is not proposing that they act as Sith, to which Yoda wisely replies, "Few do, at first. A small step the one that determines destiny often is."[21]

To assassinate Dooku, they send Jedi Quinlan Vos to team up with Dooku's former apprentice, Asajj Ventress. Things go terribly wrong, but at the end of the novel Asajj saves Vos and helps him come back from the dark side. The Jedi Council is mostly indifferent to her heroic actions, but in a show of great wisdom, Obi-Wan addresses the Council with the following revelation and chastisement:

> "Asajj Ventress moved Vos out of harm's way, taking the full force of Dooku's force lightning upon herself," Kenobi said. "She sacrificed her life to save him." "That is commendable," Mace Windu had said. "For her to give up her life for another speaks well of her." But Kenobi was shaking his auburn head. An odd, unspeakably kind smile was on his face. "You misunderstand, Master Windu, all of you. She didn't just save his life, she saved *Quinlan*, and I believe she may have saved us. ... We lost our way," Kenobi had said. "We lost it when we decided to use assassination, a practice so clearly of the dark side, for our own ends. Good intentioned though it might have been, all that has happened since: Vos succumbing to the dark side, the deaths he has directly and indirectly caused, the secrets leaked, the worlds placed in jeopardy, all of this can be traced back to that single decision. Masters I submit to you that Vos's fall was of our making, and Asajj Ventress's death is on all our hands. That Vos is here with us today, devastated but on the light path once more, is no credit to us, but to her. She died a true friend of the Jedi, and I believe that she deserves to be laid to rest with respect and care with all gratitude for the life she gave and the life she has restored to us. And this bitter

lesson that came at so dear a price, we are Jedi, and we must, all of us always, remember what that means."[22]

As the Jedi see only in the end, the decision to attempt to achieve a good end (the removal of Dooku) through evil means (assassination) was wrong, and the consequences help to illustrate this. In this strong example we see Catholic morality affirmed, as well as a warning about corruption. Nevertheless, our universe is ultimately God's Kingdom, and we have the promise the Church will never be fully corrupted, for Jesus assured, "the gates of the netherworld shall not prevail against it" (Mt 16:18).

BC and BBY

Star Wars chronology dates itself before and after the momentous conclusion of *A New Hope*, the destruction of the first Death Star. Thus, everything that occurs after that event in galactic standard years ascends numerically with the ABY appendage, signifying "After the Battle of Yavin" (Yavin being the planetary system in which the Rebel base was located and the Death Star destroyed). All events prior are in descending galactic standard years with the BBY appendage, meaning "Before the Battle of Yavin." This is very similar to the Christian usage of BC and AD, whereby we mark our historical years based on the life of the most significant person of history, Jesus of Nazareth.

Using the Force: *Star Wars* and Catholicism

Canons

Even the idea of the new Star Wars "canon" is plucked straight from Christian terminology and history. In the first century AD, the New Testament was written as individual books and letters. It would take three centuries of discussion among the early Christians about which of these books and letters, among the dozens of potential ones floating around, was inspired by God and therefore sacred. It was the authoritative body of Bishops, the successors to the apostles themselves, instituted by Christ, who decided which books and letters would be part of the 27 books in the New Testament canon, as well as which books were apocryphal (not of Divine inspiration), such as the "Shepherd of Hermas" and the various Gnostic gospels.

Similarly, as discussed in the introduction, the first few decades of *Star Wars* witnessed a central authority of storytelling (the films), surrounded by additional stories of varying authoritative weight from books, comics, games, and the like. As of Disney's acquisition of Lucasfilm and the establishment of the authoritative body—the Story Group, whose job it is to maintain continuity among all *Star Wars* property—we have a list of official canon material. All other material has been branded as "Legends." With the Story Group acting as a kind of authoritative Magisterium, the new canon material like the official Biblical canon, and the Legends material resembling apocryphal writings, we have yet another connection between *Star Wars* and Catholicism.

---

[1] Kevin Hearne, *Star Wars: Heir to the Jedi*, Audiobook narrated by Marc Thompson (Random House Audio, 2015).

[2] John C. McDowell, *The Gospel According to Star Wars: Faith, Hope, and the Force* (Louisville, Westminster John Knox Press, 2007), 18.

[3] Roy M. Anker, *Catching Light: Looking for God in the Movies* (Grand Rapids, MI: William B. Eerdmans Publishing Company, 2004), 225.

[4] Dick Staub, *Christian Wisdom of the Jedi Masters* (San Francisco: John Wiley & Sons, 2005), 75.

[5] Russell W. Dalton, *Faith Journey Through Fantasy Lands: A Christian Dialogue with Harry Potter, Star Wars, and The Lord of the Rings* (Minneapolis: Augsburg Books, 2003), 50.

[6] Anker, 239.

[7] Dalton, 62.

[8] Timothy Paul Jones, *Finding God in a Galaxy Far, Far Away: A Spiritual Exploration of the Star Wars Saga* (Sisters, OR: Multnomah, 2005), 67.

[9] Dalton, 65.

[10] Jones, 106.

[11] "40 Years of Star Wars Panel," Lucasfilm Ltd. (Star Wars Celebration Orlando, 13 April 2017) https://www.youtube.com/watch?v=YI5QodTtlME (accessed 22 July 2017).

[12] Jones, 108.

[13] Jones, 110-111.

[14] Mary Henderson, *Star Wars: The Magic of Myth* (New York: Bantam, 1997), 88.

[15] McDowell, 101.

[16] Caleb Grimes, *Star Wars Jesus: A Spiritual Commentary on the Reality of the Force* (Enumclaw, WA: WinePress Publishing, 2007), 132.

[17] Ibid.

[18] *Ultimate Star Wars* (New York: DK Penguin Random House, 2015), 63.

[19] McDowell, 82.

[20] *Catechism of the Catholic Church*, 2d ed. (Citta del Vaticano: Libreria Editrice Vaticana, 1997), § 1753.

[21] Christie Golden, *Star Wars: Dark Disciple*, Audiobook narrated by Marc Thompson (Random House Audio, 2015), 18:09.

[22] Ibid., 10:56:33.

Chapter 10: Pitfalls of *Star Wars*

"I have a bad feeling about this."
– Running gag throughout *Star Wars*

"It's a trap!"
– Admiral Ackbar (*Return of the Jedi*)

As with most things in life, since *Star Wars* is not perfectly correlated with Catholicism, there are some areas of concern. It is worthwhile to be aware of these so as to avoid false ideologies. Religious researcher and Christian, Joshua Hays, posits:

> The proper response to the implicit theology and worldview of Star Wars is neither boycott

nor wholesale embrace. Paul encourages believers to "hate what is evil" but to "cling to what is good" (Rom 12:9). To reject the movies outright is to deprive oneself of important lessons about justice, truth, and reconciliation, not to mention the simple joy of a good story. On the other hand, however, John charges Christians to "test the spirits to see whether they are from God" (1 John 4:1). Active discernment is required to identify the worldview advocated by the Jedi masters and evaluate it according to the word of God.[1]

This chapter will explore the potential pitfalls in order to aid those who wish to understand *Star Wars* in a spiritually healthy way.

Logical Inconsistencies

Unfortunately, *Star Wars* is littered with all sorts of logical inconsistencies. One example comes right at the epic climax of *Revenge of the Sith*. While conversing on the landing platform on Mustafar, Anakin says, "If you're not with me, then you're my enemy," to which Obi-Wan replies, "Only a Sith deals in absolutes. I will do what I must." Here Anakin echoes language of Jesus in Matthew 12:30, "Whoever is not with me is against me." The troubling statement, though, is Obi-Wan's, because it is contradictory even to Jedi ideology.

Jedi repeatedly deal in absolutes, including this very statement, "Only a Sith deals in absolutes," thereby rendering it self-contradictory. Just moments later in the heat of battle, Obi-Wan makes another absolute statement, "Anakin, Chancellor Palpatine is evil." Hays highlights other examples among the Jedi:

> Absolute statements have surrounded Anakin since his discovery as the prophesied Chosen One on Tatooine. Upon his return to Coruscant, Qui-Gon Jinn tells the Jedi Council, "Finding him was the will of the Force. I have no doubt of that."[2]

Furthermore, Hays argues, "Most of Yoda's instructions to Luke in the ways of the Force are absolute statements, including classic lines like 'Do, or do not. There is no try,' and 'Size matters not.'"[3]

Another inconsistency is Yoda's claim during Luke's training in *The Empire Strikes Back*: "Once you start down the dark path, forever will it dominate your destiny, consume you it will, as it did Obi-Wan's apprentice." This is not true, even in the *Star Wars* universe and Yoda's own experience as we have touched upon earlier. Redemption is certainly possible, and [SPOILER for *Dark Disciple* novel in this sentence] a person may return from the dark side as Yoda saw accomplished with Asajj Ventress and more closely with Jedi Quinlan Vos.

The film *Return of the Jedi* proves Yoda's teaching false when Anakin too is redeemed and "returns" as a Jedi. Catholicism agrees that all people have the possibility of redemption until death. Perhaps Yoda is trying to be safe with Luke—suggesting a turn to darkness is irrevocable, even though he knows this is false—because of the volatility in Luke's character. Hays agrees: "My suspicion is that Yoda knows as much but overstates his point out of concern for

Skywalker's future."[4] The point here is that the philosophy operative within *Star Wars* is not always internally consistent, which is why it is a potential pitfall.

Commanding the Force

One common objection against *Star Wars* is that the Jedi and Sith command the Force to do their will, whereas no Christian commands God but rather bends to God's will. I believe this objection is more true of the Sith than of the Jedi, because the Jedi seem to work by flowing with the Force, seeking its will and working with it, rather than what the Sith do; they seem to distort the Force in an attempt to bend it to their desires, even coaxing it. The Sith and dark side users are more like witches or sorcerers in their desire to conjure dark force power, and it is to *Star Wars*' credit that this type of activity is related to the dark side only.

Considering to what degree the Jedi "use" the force, we ought to consider Luke's training. Obi-Wan Kenobi instructs Luke saying, "A Jedi can feel the Force flowing through him" (*A New Hope*). Luke responds, "You mean it controls your actions?" Obi-Wan retorts, "Partially. But it also obeys your commands." Frequently, both Jedi and Sith use the Force to do marvelous things like moving objects, "seeing" without physical eyesight, and suggesting thoughts in people's minds, perhaps somewhat like hypnotism. This is not foreign to Catholicism, because many mystical things occur within our tradition. For example, Saints have been known to possess the gifts of levitation, bilocation (where they appear to be present physically in more than one place simultaneously), and an ability to read souls in the confessional. The Spirit provides graces to do supernatural things at times. Therefore, if we are willing to receive the graces of the Spirit, it may influence our actions, like the Force.

As far as Jedi "commanding" the Force, we must remember Jesus promised the Spirit will obey commands: "If you have faith the size of a mustard seed, you will say to this mountain, 'Move from here to there,' and it will move. Nothing will be impossible for you" (Mt 17:20). Jesus also said, "Whatever you ask in my name, I will do" (Jn 14:13). Christians do wield a power like the Jedi. Through the Spirit, Catholic clergy forgive sins, instill people with graces, change their souls forever through sacraments, and transubstantiate bread and wine into the flesh and blood of Jesus.

Yoda tells Luke in *The Empire Strikes Back* that one may discern the good side from the bad "when you are calm, at peace, passive." In Christianity, a person at peace, meditative, and in contemplative prayer may well discern the will of God. Both the Jedi and the Christian are encouraged to live in harmony with the light or God. For a Jedi to command the light side of the Force to do something against its will would be counter to the Jedi's relationship with the Force, much like a Christian would not go against the will of God. Therefore, I see little concern for the way Jedi interact with the Force and "use" it. In fact, it seems to be the will of the Force that the Jedi do use it for good, just as God wills Catholics to use our charisms, or special gifts of the Holy Spirit (see 1 Cor 12).

Anthony Digmann

The Dark Side are They

Anger, fear, aggression, and hate are listed as dark side qualities, and this necessitates some clarification from a Christian perspective. While hate is bad, the other three are not inherently evil. Hays comments:

> Anger, fear, and aggression are all certainly volatile feelings to be managed with caution, but they are not necessarily negative as Yoda claims. Instead, they are ordinary experiences of human beings living within a fallen world alongside other imperfect people.[5]

As a human, Jesus would have experienced each of these, just like everyone in the *Star Wars* galaxy; however, the important point is our reaction to these emotions in thought as well as deed. Even Jesus experienced holy and justified anger when he drove the moneychangers from the Temple. We are also to have a healthy fear of the Lord, an awe of his majesty and glory. Hays continues, "They are not themselves sinful by any means, but they are less than what God intended for his people in a perfect world. Although Yoda was wrong to label these feelings as the dark side, he was right to warn of their peril."[6] In *Dark Disciple*, Asajj Ventress correctly notes there is a big difference between *feeling* dark side emotions and *using* them.[7] In *The Phantom Menace* we hear Yoda "describe these feelings as *the path* to the dark side, not the dark side itself," explains Hays.[8] This improves Yoda's position on the issue when he states, "Fear is the path to the dark side. Fear leads to anger. Anger leads to hate. Hate leads to suffering."[9] Thus, the prequel films provide a more theologically accurate position as Yoda sees anger, fear, and aggression as *paths* to the dark side, not the dark side themselves.

Salvation

While *Star Wars* offers numerous examples of self-sacrifice and "saviors" reminiscent of Christ, no self-sacrificing hero in the franchise perfectly mimics the salvation offered by Jesus, and some instances lead to potential heresy. James Papandrea notes that *Star Wars* includes a lot of self-saving, which is motivated by seeing the self-sacrifice of others. "In Arianism, it is not the death of the savior that saves you; it is your response to the savior's death and your willingness to follow in the savior's footsteps," he writes.[10] "Anyone may *become* a savior by following that example and responding appropriately to the previous savior."[11]

While this is largely true regarding the reversion and self-sacrificing heroism of Vader, it is not true for all characters. [SPOILERS in this paragraph.] The deaths of many characters involve a self-sacrifice offered for others in which the hero who dies is not saving themselves such as Obi-Wan, Kanan Jarrus, Asajj Ventress, and even Luke Skywalker in *The Last Jedi*. Sometimes these deaths have a redeeming quality on behalf of a character who has lost his or her way, such as Ventress and Skywalker, but their sacrifice still resembles Christ.

Papandrea is accurate to say there is no figure in *Star Wars* who achieves salvation for all in the way Jesus does for all humanity, but the sacrifices of heroes in the franchise resemble the selfless-love of Christ and inspire in the audience the value of being similarly self-sacrificial. While we are unable to save the universe, we may act *like* Christ to save others in a finite way, which may also include reparation for our own personal sins. *Star Wars* is replete with such examples. The caution is to be aware of how elements of the franchise may lead to heretical problems, even though it remains largely consistent with many Christian values.

Relativism

Another concern levied against *Star Wars* is that it promotes moral relativism. Moral relativism is the fallacious idea there is no true good or evil but that each person may determine what is right or wrong for themselves. Relativism is also self-refuting, because it proposes there are no objective moral standards that apply to everyone—a statement that in itself is a moral standard meant to apply to everyone. Catholics are not relativists; we believe in objective truth, and we make statements that express objective truth.

Several examples of relativistic thought in *Star Wars* have been proposed. After Yoda's death in *Return of the Jedi*, Luke encounters Obi-Wan as a Force ghost and confronts him about the identity of Darth Vader. Previously, Obi-Wan told Luke that Vader "betrayed and murdered your father," failing to reveal the full truth that Vader *was* Luke's father (*A New Hope*). Obi-Wan's response when confronted is, "What I told you was true, from a certain point of view," and, "Luke, you're going to find that many of the truths we cling to depend greatly on our own point of view." This proposal may be taken by viewers to the extreme of relativism, even though within *Star Wars* good and evil are clear.

We witness Sidious using this perspective to tempt Anakin in the Galaxies Opera House in *Revenge of the Sith* when he says, "Good is a point of view." We would expect relativism to be justified by a Sith; however, Jedi also use this type of reasoning. For instance, frustrated with the Council's decision rejecting Anakin's training as a Jedi in *The Phantom Menace*, Qui-Gon Jinn listens to Obi-Wan defend "the Council's decision to his master, saying, 'It is not disrespect, master, it is the truth,'" to which Qui-Gon replies, "From your point of view."[12]

Star Wars presents another logical inconsistency here, because it affirms good vs. evil and light vs. dark, but it occasionally offers these morally relativistic ideas, which are characteristic of a Sith but problematic from a Jedi. We can see the consequences for Qui-Gon's defiant actions because he has not yet been promoted to the Council. We may be able to explain away Obi-Wan's misdirection about Luke's father in *A New Hope* as being in Luke's best interests at the time. Perhaps he was not yet ready for the full truth. Nevertheless, Obi-Wan's defense of his half-truths in *Return of the Jedi* is not helpful and risks traversing the path of relativism.

Relativistic ideas come not only from *Star Wars* under George Lucas but also from recent material. An example of relativistic thought from a 2017 novel actually quotes from the *Journal of the Whills*, a type of holy book from the *Star Wars* Galaxy, "The truth in our soul is that nothing is true. The question of life is what then do we do? The burden is ours. To penance, we hew. The Force binds us all from a certain point of view."[13] Notice the use of the "point of view" phrase again. The most problematic statement here, though, is the first sentence. The claim that "nothing is true" is a pure relativistic statement, and the fact that it comes from a source as important as the *Journal of the Whills* is highly significant, as well as detrimental to the logical consistency of the spirituality of the Force.

The franchise would be far better off maintaining true intellectual and moral objectivity for all light characters and only allow dark side users to dabble with moral relativism. [SPOILER] One such example of the Sith employing moral relativism is when Count Dooku is trying to turn Jedi Quinlan Vos into a Sith in *Dark Disciple*. He says, "There is no good or evil, only those with power and those without it."[14] That is fitting for a Sith, but not for the Jedi.

Despite this, the franchise repeatedly counters its own occasional relativism. Clearly, Anakin's turn to the dark side in *Revenge of the Sith* is not morally ambiguous, as if it were justified by Anakin's new "point-of-view" that the Jedi are evil. Obi-Wan is right to say, "Then, you are lost," to Anakin, because Anakin's thinking has reversed.

Even in very difficult moral situations, objective moral truth is heroically upheld. In the *Lords of the Sith* novel [SPOILERS for the next two paragraphs], for example, a group of Twi'leks under the command of Cham Syndulla on their home planet of Ryloth are tracking Darth Vader and the Emperor through the jungle in an attempt to kill them. Vader and the Emperor were vulnerable to attack at one point when resting in a village of primitive Twi'leks. Cham and his lieutenant, Isval, had the opportunity to call in an airstrike of Imperial ships under Cham's influence to take out Vader and the Emperor, knowing most of the village would be wiped out as well. They argue about the best course-of-action:

"Think about what we're considering here," Cham said. "Having V-wings strafe a village of Twi'leks. Imperial pilots killing Twi'leks on our orders. That's what we're talking about. Think about that." Isval didn't have to think about it. Cham's words hit her like a punch. ... She'd been convinced that strafing the village was the right thing to do, that killing Twi'leks was worth it to get at Vader. Her skin warmed with shame and she bowed her head. "It's alright," Cham said to her. She looked up at him. "No it's not." "We all lose ourselves sometimes, Isval," he said. "We just have to find our way back." And all at once she was reminded why Cham was so important to the [Free Ryloth] movement and whatever came after. He'd fought the Empire for years, hated what the Empire stood for, no less than she did, but always his hate and his methods were informed by his principles.[15]

Cham represents the fact that the end does not justify the means, while Isval shows eventual obedience to her conscience and eventual prudent reasoning from natural law. Cham and Isval had been executing an elaborate plan to kill these two ultra-powers of the Empire the whole length of the book, exhausting incredible resources and lives in the process. However, even when Cham has the two highest priority targets in the whole galaxy at his mercy, he refuses to take the shot, because it will also mean the deaths of innocents. Cham knows such action would be morally evil. This is a profound testimony to moral character, and Cham is regarded as being a first-rate commander as a result of his principles. While the *Star Wars* franchise has elements of relativism, it has far more objective morality, and scenes like this are worth noting for inspiration and instruction.

Another line from Obi-Wan Kenobi is worth exploring. In *A New Hope*, Obi-Wan tells Luke he must come to Alderaan to learn the ways of the Force and become a Jedi, but Luke declines the offer. Obi-Wan responds, "You must do what you feel is right, of course." Moral relativists may be quick to use this line in their favor; however, something different seems to be at work. Hays suggests, "Obi-Wan entrusts Luke to make the right decision. His remark is not a comment of resignation but an invitation. ... He gently pushes Luke to make a decision, but when the youth balks, Obi-Wan does not insist on the issue."[16]

Obi-Wan is playing his hand carefully and treading lightly at this point. Hays concludes, "Christians can surprisingly learn from Obi-Wan's example about how to share Jesus with a postmodern culture."[17] We ought to evangelize by invitation, not pushing. This was Christ's *modus operandi* after all. As Catholics, just as God has given us free will and respects our exercise of that gift, we also strive to respect the free will of our contemporaries, though we pray their decisions will be made with well-formed consciences in accord with objective truth.

Pluralism

Similar to the concern of relativism is the worldview of pluralism. Pluralism is the belief that all religions are equal, true in their own way, and have something to offer human understanding of the spiritual realm. Often this also means that even the sum total of all religious truth, gathered from all religions, would still not be all the truth, as if there is still more to discover. Pluralism borders on the idea of religious relativism, which suggests there is no religious truth in any objective sense.

Both of these ideas are erroneous, because objective truth is real for everyone in all places, at all times. Christians believe the truths revealed by God not merely because they like them or were enlightened by them in meditation, but because they were revealed to humanity by the one and only God of the universe. The pluralist who says God reveals different truths to different religions runs into the overwhelming problem of having to deal with inconsistencies between religions, making them mutually exclusive.

For example, Christians say Jesus Christ is the second person of the Trinity, the incarnate and divine Son of God who came to earth, suffered, was crucified, died, resurrected from the dead, and ascended into heaven. Other religions, even those closest to Christianity like Judaism and Islam, reject these beliefs on a fundamental level. These beliefs about Jesus cannot be both true and false. Christians and others cannot both be right—either Jesus is who we believe he is or he is not. Pluralism and religious relativism lead to all sorts of similar problems.

At the opposite end of the spectrum from relativism is exclusivism. An exclusivist believes him or herself to be right and all other opposing views to be wrong. Such a perspective is held by some Christian communities and religions; however, it is considered by most to be intolerant and arrogant. Exclusivism fails to see the good present in other ideologies. Even St. Paul testifies,

"Test everything, retain what is good" (1 Thess 5:21), thus implying good in other ideologies.

The worldview held by Catholicism is inclusivism. This perspective recognizes truth in all religions; however, it also understands its position as the truest. Rather than saying "What I believe is true, and everyone else is wrong or believes something false," the inclusivist says, "What I believe is the fullness of truth, and others possess varying elements of the truth, depending upon their alignment with objective truth." The *Catechism of the Catholic Church* teaches that Catholicism alone possesses the fullness of truth revealed by God through Jesus Christ in the following passage:

> The Second Vatican Council's *Decree on Ecumenism* explains: "For it is through Christ's Catholic Church *alone*, which is the universal help toward salvation, that the *fullness of the means of salvation* can be obtained [emphasis mine]. It was to the apostolic college alone, of which Peter is the head, that we believe that our Lord entrusted all the blessings of the New Covenant, in order to establish on earth the one Body of Christ into which all those should be fully incorporated who belong in any way to the People of God.[18]

This doesn't exclude truth in other religions, it simply affirms Catholicism has been given and maintains truth in its purest form.

Nevertheless, the Church appreciates legitimate diversity and also affirms that "'many elements of sanctification and of truth' are found outside the visible confines of the Catholic Church."[19] Thus, while Catholicism is the truest religion, others share in the truth to varying degrees. Officially,

> The Catholic Church recognizes in other religions that search, among shadows and images, for the God who is unknown yet near since he gives life and breath and all things and wants all men to be saved. Thus, the Church considers all goodness and truth found in these religions as "a preparation for the Gospel and given by him who enlightens all men that they may at length have life."[20]

Lucas speaks from a pluralistic perspective in his personal beliefs. When asked what he thinks about people reading religion into *Star Wars*, Lucas replied:

> I don't see *Star Wars* as profoundly religious, I see *Star Wars* as taking all of the issues that religion represents and trying to distill them down into a more modern and more easily accessible construct that people can grab onto to accept the fact that there is a greater mystery out there. When I was 10 years old I asked my mother, I said, "Well, there's only one God, why are there so many religions?" and over the years I've been pondering that question ever since, and it would seem to me that the conclusion I've come to is that all the religions are true, they just see a different part of the elephant. A religion is basically a container for faith. Faith is the glue that holds us together as a society, faith in our culture, our world, you know whatever it is

we're trying to hang onto, is a very important part of allowing us to remain stable, remain balanced.[21]

When he says "all religions are true," but with varying perspectives, he is espousing pluralism—an unfortunately common religious thought of postmodernism. It should be no surprise that his view leaked into the films, but we ought to recognize this and call its errors to the attention of others when necessary.

Merely One Myth among Many

It should be noted that Christianity is included in Joseph Campbell's research (discussed in "Chapter 2: *Star Wars* Origins"). Therein, Campbell reduced Christianity to one story among many—regardless of its historical and archaeological corroboration—a pitfall we must avoid. Campbell's amalgamation of mythological motifs has some use, as we have seen its ability to resonate universally through *Star Wars*; however, Catholicism is not merely another myth among many.

Joseph Campbell falls into inestimable error by lacking discernment of truth and fiction in his study of myths. He once wrote, "We do not particularly care whether Rip van Winkle, Kamar al-Zaman or Jesus Christ ever actually lived. Their stories are what concern us."[22] What a tragic oversight! There may be academic benefit to distilling the common threads from various cultural tales into similar themes and plot structures as Campbell has done; however, such an exercise misses the immensity of spiritual truth and significance among the tales that are actually, historically real. Such an error as Campbell's is worse than a Jedi who completely ignores the Force and instead spends his or her time focused merely on an exhaustive study of various lightsaber combat forms and styles.

Unlike other myths, Christian belief about Jesus has historical and archaeological evidence to support it. For a comprehensive, scholarly treatment of the evidence for the Resurrection having actually occurred in history, see N.T. Wright's *The Resurrection of the Son of God* (Fortress Press, 2003), for example. Yet, in our culture, many people would equate all myths as fable. It may be helpful to recognize the difference between myth and theology as Stephen May explains, "Theology is language 'about' God based on the language 'of' God — that is, given to us by God so that we may speak about him accurately."[23] On the other hand, "Mythology, by contrast, consists of stories we invent off the top of our own heads to try and make sense of a puzzling universe."[24] When we speak of Christianity as myth, we recognize that it shares some of the same elements we find in fables from human cultures and constructs, but ultimately we recognize it is different, because it is from Divine Revelation and actually occurred in history.

This was true for C.S. Lewis, the acclaimed Christian author of the mythologically saturated Christian allegory *The Chronicles of Narnia*. Hays explains:

> After decades of studying medieval literature, C. S. Lewis came to faith through the recognition that the story of Jesus is the "true myth." The biblical tale of a dying and rising God was

familiar to Lewis from his studies of world mythologies "but with this tremendous difference that *it really happened.*"[25]

A consumer of *Star Wars* ought to be aware that Christianity is no mere equal myth among many, and that we have evidence to support this claim.

The only mythmaker of the past century to rival Lucas's grand story is devout Catholic, J. R. R. Tolkien, the mastermind behind *The Lord of the Rings*. On the subject of myth, he believes the "one true myth" of Christ has echoes in all other fictional myths of humanity. Tolkien explains:

> We have come from God...[so] inevitably the myths woven by us, though they contain error, reflect a splintered fragment of the true light, the eternal truth that is with God. Myths may be misguided, but they steer however shakily toward the true harbor.[26]

Christian pastor, Timothy Paul Jones further comments on mythology and Christianity: "Every unexpected hero is a distant echo of the virgin-born boy from Galilee; every sacrificial twist is a whisper of the Cross; and every triumphant turn to victory is a misty reflection of the Resurrection."[27] In such ways, myths lead us to the truth of Christ.

Sexuality

I have always appreciated that *Star Wars* has remained fairly family friendly when it comes to sexuality. The most concerning elements in the first six films are occasional displays of immodesty in attire, such as Leia's slave bikini in Jabba's Palace. Even in that instance though, it is not portrayed as good, but rather as an evil enslavement and objectification of Leia by Jabba. The strongest sexual involvement I have encountered involves fornication (i.e., sexual relations of an unmarried man and woman) between the main characters of the *Lost Stars* novel. The two scenes in the book are far from graphic, more on the level of a PG-13 film. Nonetheless, the book is marketed to young readers, and I believe it is important to be clear with youth about God's plan for sexuality. These two sinful interludes are not condemned in the novel and do not bear negative repercussions, thereby offering no deterrent, pause, or concern related to the sin of fornication. Rather than promoting traditional sexual moral norms, the book seems to assume fornication is normative, like almost all of contemporary media. It is worth forming our children well with regard to all media and helping them call into question inappropriate material.

An additional concern is that homosexuality has begun appearing in some of the novels. Like fornication, some authors seem to be taking homosexual activity as normative. As Catholics we cannot approve of any sexual action other than by one man and one woman who are married and objectively open to life, promoting both the unitive and procreative purposes of the sexual act. I have yet to encounter a situation in which homosexuality is praised, though. Rather, it seems to be simply mentioned. For example, young Temmin "Snap" Wexley's aunt and caregiver in Chuck Wendig's *Aftermath* is a lesbian with a live-in partner. The most prominent character in Wendig's novel trilogy with same-sex attraction is the ex-Imperial, Sinjir Rath Velus. In the *Ahsoka* novel, a female friend of Ahsoka Tano comments that she could kiss Ahsoka—a sexual advance which leaves Ahsoka speechless.[28] The female friend recognizes potential "Jedi hangups" Ahsoka may have, which would prevent such an exchange but offers it nonetheless, almost involuntarily, on a spur of the moment. Finally, a female Moff in *Lords of the Sith* is also openly homosexual, yet in her case, she is portrayed in morally unfavorable light. A general acceptance of homosexual activity is common in our culture, so it may be no surprise to see it in *Star Wars* novels as well. However, none of these examples adds to the story; the sexual orientation serves these storylines in no practical way.

Instilling God's vision for human sexuality into youth and respecting it as adults is incredibly important. The Catholic Church has wonderful resources to this end, such as Pope St. John Paul II's *Theology of the Body*. When popular media promotes ideologies in conflict with God's vision, it becomes problematic. Yet again we find another example of the need to be clear about God's plan for moral living. It will be useful for parents and educators to be aware of such questionable material in the *Star Wars* franchise, just as in all elements of contemporary media.

Eastern Religions and Occultism

Some Christians have expressed a concern about *Star Wars* leading youth into Eastern religious thought or occultism. As we have explored at length, the films are based on common threads from mythologies across time and the globe. Its source material is vast, which is why it resonates internationally. There are Eastern elements at times, such as when we discover in Yoda's meditating chamber he has a fountain, singing stones, and heated oils.[29] While there are Eastern inspired elements, core messages and themes of the films fit Christian values well. Furthermore, the Church recognizes truth in all world religions, so following St. Paul's advice once more is prudent, "Test everything; retain what is good" (1 Thess 5:21).

On the topic of Occultism, there is use of dark magick in the franchise. The most poignant I have seen is with the Nightsisters on Dathomir, led by Mother Talzin, principally found in a couple of *The Clone Wars* episodes. They are literally involved with conjuring deceased clan members, sorcery, magick, voodoo, and the like. The evil coercion of spiritual powers is a reality with occult groups in our world, so, unlike the fictional lightsaber wielding Sith, this topic deserves special attention.

The Judeo-Christian tradition has always been opposed to occult activity like witchcraft. Scripture makes clear:

> Let there not be found among you anyone who causes their son or daughter to pass through the fire, or practices divination, or is a soothsayer, augur, or sorcerer, or who casts spells, consults ghosts and spirits, or seeks oracles from the dead. Anyone who does such things is an abomination to the LORD (Deut 18:10-12).

Among the many evils committed by King Manasseh in the *Bible*: "He practiced soothsaying and divination, and reintroduced the consulting of ghosts and spirits. He did much evil in the Lord's sight and provoked him to anger" (2 Chr 33:6). The consequences were quite severe for such abominations, as God takes such evil very seriously: "You shall not let a woman who practices sorcery live" (Ex 22:11). Since the Nightsisters mimic real occult activity, we ought to use such examples from *Star Wars* as "teaching moments" to share the truth of God's condemnation of occult activity.

To the credit of *Star Wars*, such dark side users are seen as evil, though viewers may at times sympathize with them, [SPOILERS in this paragraph] such as when the Nightsisters are slaughtered by a Separatist army led by General Grievous. The closest we come to seeing dark side activity portrayed as good is in the novel *Dark Disciple*. Therein, Asajj Ventress is training Jedi Quinlan Vos in the nature of the dark side in order for them to assassinate Count Dooku. Frequently, the reader is in a position to sympathize with the moral ambiguity of their plan. However, the negative consequences of such dark dabbling, as well as the morally questionable means of using assassination to eliminate Dooku, become clear throughout the book. Ultimately, evil is recognized as evil and good is recognized as good, though such a story may not be appropriate for the immature reader who may confuse truths with fantasy.

Fantasy Indulgence

Another concern is that this mythology can lead to an over-indulgence in the franchise and in fantasy in general. It is no secret decades after his involvement with *Star Wars*, Sir Alec Guinness had misgivings about it. He explains:

Using the Force: *Star Wars* and Catholicism

Twenty years ago, when the film was first shown, it had a freshness, also a sense of moral good and fun. Then I began to be uneasy about the influence it might be having. The bad penny first dropped in San Francisco when a sweet-faced boy of twelve told me proudly that he had seen *Star Wars* over a hundred times. His elegant mother nodded with approval.[30]

Guinness felt this was taking it all much too far, and he is correct; the boy ought to have used his time toward much more noble pursuits. Guinness responded: "Do you think you could promise never to see *Star Wars* again?," which appalled the mother and left the boy in tears.[31] It seems the allure of Lucas's mythology had replaced in this boy's life other things, like authentic religion, which should have been the cornerstone of his upbringing. On another occasion Guinness remembers being asked by a child near the end of Mass for his autograph: "'Not here,' I replied rather crossly."[32] Guinness recognizes what is really important, and he witnesses to the truths of Catholicism.

When asked about the fact that more youth are "turning to movies for inspiration," instead of the *Bible* and Christianity, George Lucas stated:

> I think there's definitely a place for organized religion, that's a very important part of the social fabric, and I would hate to find ourselves in a completely secular world where entertainment was passing for some kind of religious experience.[33]

Unfortunately, though, this has happened for some people, and it stresses all the more a need for evangelization. When asked if he's aware of the impact his films have on youth, Lucas responded:

> I have a philosophy that we all teach, and we all teach every day of our lives, and it's not necessarily what we lecture. I've discovered that kids don't like lectures at all. But it is really the way we live our lives, and what we do with our lives and the way we conduct ourselves, and once in a while they listen to the lectures. So, when I make the films, I'm very aware of the fact that I'm teaching on a much larger scale than I would just as a parent or somebody walking through life, because I have this megaphone. Anybody in the media has a very large megaphone that they can reach a lot of different people, and so whatever they say, whatever they do, however they conduct themselves, whatever they produce has an influence and is teaching somebody something, and I try to be aware of what it is I'm saying.[34]

This resonates closely with what Pope St. Paul VI wrote in 1975: "Modern man listens more willingly to witnesses than to teachers, and if he does listen to teachers, it is because they are witnesses."[35]

I do not believe fault should be levied against Lucas or *Star Wars* for the way it is used by some people as a substitute for religion. That would be like blaming Tolkien and the *Lord of the Rings* for a similar fault. The problem is not in these modern myths but in the loss of Christianity from our personal spiritualties and our post-modern culture. It is more the fault of Christians for not keeping the Church alive and in excellent health. As Catholics, charged to share the true Gospel of Christ in the world, religious apathy is lamentable, but it is the mission field in which we live. Those attracted to *Star Wars* may be the same people trying to fulfill their longing for God and authentic religion with an alternate myth—all the more the need to evangelize through *Star Wars*.

---

[1] Joshua Hays, *A True Hope: Jedi Perils and the Way of Jesus* (Macon, GA: Smyth & Helwys, 2015), 7.

[2] Ibid., 19.

[3] Ibid.

[4] Ibid., 89.

[5] Ibid., 73.

[6] Ibid., 77.

[7] Christie Golden, *Star Wars: Dark Disciple*, Audiobook narrated by Marc Thompson (Random House Audio, 2015), 3:56:50.

[8] Hays, 77.

[9] Ibid.

[10] James L. Papandrea, *From Star Wars to Superman: Christ Figures in Science Fiction and Superhero Films* (Manchester, NH: Sophia Institute Press, 2017), 76.

[11] Ibid.

[12] Hays, 120.

[13] Chuck Wendig, *Star Wars Aftermath: Empire's End*, Audiobook narrated by Marc Thompson (Random House Audio, 2017), 6:38:25.

[14] Golden, 6:18:10.

[15] Paul S. Kemp, *Star Wars: Lords of the Sith*, Audiobook narrated by Jonathan Davis (Random House Audio, 2015), 10:14:30.

[16] Hays, 132.

[17] Ibid.

[18] *Catechism of the Catholic Church*, 2d ed. (Citta del Vaticano: Libreria Editrice Vaticana, 1997), § 816.

[19] Ibid., § 819.

[20] Ibid., § 843.

[21] Bill Moyers, *The Mythology of Star Wars with George Lucas and Bill Moyers* (Public Affairs Television, Inc., 1999), https://vimeo.com/groups/183185/videos/38026023 (accessed 21 July 2017).

[22] David Wilkinson, *The Power of the Force: the Spirituality of the Star Wars Films* (Oxford: Lion, 2000), 149.

[23] Ibid., 147.

[24] Ibid.

[25] Hays, 130.

[26] Timothy Paul Jones, *Finding God in a Galaxy Far, Far Away: A Spiritual Exploration of the Star Wars Saga* (Sisters, OR: Multnomah, 2005), 21.

[27] Ibid., 137.

[28] E. K. Johnston, *Star Wars: Ahsoka*, Audiobook narrated by Ashley Eckstein (Random House Audio, 2016), approximately 6:30:30.

[29] Golden, 8:59:15.

[30] Sir Alec Guinness, *A Positively Final Appearance: A Journal 1996-1998* (New York: Viking, 1999), 11.

[31] Ibid.

[32] Ibid., 12.

[33] Bill Moyers, *The Mythology of Star Wars with George Lucas and Bill Moyers* (Public Affairs Television, Inc., 1999), https://vimeo.com/groups/183185/videos/38026023 (accessed 21 July 2017).

[34] Ibid.

[35] Pope Paul VI, *Evangelii Nuntiandi* (8 December 1975) http://w2.vatican.va/content/paul-vi/en/apost_exhortations/documents/hf_p-vi_exh_19751208_evangelii-nuntiandi.html (accessed 25 October 2017), 41.

Conclusion

"Pass on what you have learned."
– Yoda (*Return of the Jedi*)

As a child I would have been thrilled to live in the *Star Wars* galaxy and serve as a Jedi Knight. The fantasy adventure of it all captivated me, and I wanted to belong to something of significance, to do good and change the world. I would have been honored to stand among my fellow Jedi, wielding a lightsaber in combat against an evil foe or flying a starfighter in a great galactic battle. As I have reflected on the *Star Wars* franchise as an adult, I am insurmountably thankful I live in our real universe instead of the *Star Wars* fantasy universe, even if I were a Jedi Knight rather than some peon in that galaxy far, far away. This is for simple reasons such as the state of Galactic politics, Empire conspirators (original Empire and thereafter the First Order), and crime syndicates, which coalesce into a more turbulent existence than I enjoy. There are also practical reasons, like I appreciate my arms and legs and know from experience with toys that I should never be allowed to handle a real lightsaber. Yet, there are more significant reasons that help me appreciate reality over the fantasy of *Star Wars*.

Connecting to the Sacred

The first major reason I appreciate our universe is that we all may have a relationship with God. In *Star Wars*, all living things are connected with the Force; however, those who have power to wield the Force need to be Force sensitive and trained to use it. There is some correlation here, because priests, for example, need training and ordination in order to work great spiritual feats such as the sacraments. However, in our real universe the invitation is open to everyone to come to know God more deeply. We may connect with God through prayer and the sacraments, as well as develop charisms and other gifts of the Holy Spirit with which God has willed to bless us, regardless of our "Force sensitivity."

With new canon material under Disney's ownership we are learning about some beings from *Star Wars* that are not Force sensitive, yet have a devotion to the Force. Thus, it is becoming a bit more like reality. For instance, there is a group of people who are members of the "Church of the Force." One such member is Lor San Tekka in *The Force Awakens*, the old man with the map to Luke. Tekka "uncovered many fragments of ancient Jedi traditions that the Old Empire had worked so hard to destroy. When Luke Skywalker began researching Jedi history in the hope of restoring the Jedi Order, he learned much from Lor San Tekka."[1] Maz Kanata too, though neither a Jedi nor member of the Church of the

Force, "has a strong connection to the Force," according to an official source.² In *Catalyst: A* Rogue One *Novel*, Jyn Erso's mother, Lyra, is Force-sensitive in the literal sense. She lacks the ability to use it like the Jedi, but she can sense things through the Force.³

We see another example of an opening of the Force to "laypeople" in the *Aftermath: Empire's End* novel. A doubting young man named Addar, who is apparently the son of the woman who founded the Church of the Force, asked another member of the Church of the Force (Jumon) about his faith in the Force. Jumon says he had an experience in which he was guided by the Force, to which Addar replies, "You're lying. The Force is only for the Jedi." Jumon corrects Addar, "They wield it, but the Force is in all living things. It is what gives us our intuition, our drive, it's what connects us to one another. We are all one with the Force."⁴

In reality we have additional profound, tangible ways of connecting with God absent from *Star Wars*. For example, through the sacraments we are filled with God's grace and share in his life. In the most profound of the sacraments, the Eucharist, we enjoy union with God himself. The Incarnation of Jesus, God become man, is another tangible thing in our universe far better than anything in *Star Wars*. There is no incarnation of the Force in their universe, which would be a fantastic thing to behold. Certainly it is fantastic, and we can experience it here in the person of Jesus Christ.

Heaven

When we consider the death and afterlife differences between *Star Wars* and Catholicism, I believe there is no contest. From what we know in *Star*

Wars, everyone (except a handful) transforms into the Force upon death and loses consciousness. Conversely, Catholicism teaches everyone retains their consciousness after death. When we die, we will not merely be absorbed by God into his divine glory; we remain ourselves. By God's grace should we find ourselves in heaven, we will be aware of ourselves and others in his presence. Furthermore, we will be able to pray for and intercede on behalf of others who are part of the Communion of Saints. While God's will may not allow us to appear as a vision or locution to those on earth like a Force ghost, it is much more plausible to attain everlasting life with self-consciousness in reality than in the *Star Wars* universe. Even the souls who have separated themselves from God and merit eternal damnation in hell retain their consciousness. In reality, we are eternal beings from the moment of our conception who will either enjoy eternity in heaven or suffer damnation in hell. Many of us may require purification in purgatory before enjoying heaven, as nothing impure may enter heaven (see Rev 21:27), yet such souls will exist for all eternity nonetheless.

Assured Victory

A final thing I appreciate about our universe is we are certain that good will prevail and that God is stronger than all darkness combined. In *Star Wars* there exists more of a Taoist ambiguity combined with the Christian worldview. We get the sense that the will of the Force will bring the light back to the fore and remove the dark Sith from power; however, we cannot be sure. Hays comments, "After decades of struggle against the Emperor's evil, Yoda departs uncertain of the light side's victory."[5] I greatly appreciate knowing how everything will end, that all will be set right, and that God will triumph (see Mt 16:18). For these reasons I am grateful to live in reality rather than the fantasy galaxy of *Star Wars*. I will gladly give up the slim chance of being a force-wielding Jedi, with all sorts of force powers, for the opportunity to serve God in this life and hopefully enjoy the Beatific Vision of heaven for all eternity with self-awareness.

Commission

The final words of the greatest Jedi of all time, Master Yoda, were incredibly significant to Luke, and they ring true for us as well. In *Return of the Jedi*, Yoda struggles at the moment of death to tell Luke, "When gone am I, the last of the Jedi will you be. Luke, the Force runs strong in your family; pass on what you have learned. Luke, there is another Skywalker." This is Luke's great commission, and it resembles the commission given to us by our Lord who tells us: "Go, therefore, and make disciples of all nations, baptizing them in the name of the Father, and of the Son, and of the holy Spirit, teaching them to observe all that I have commanded you" (Mt 28:20).

As Jesus leaves us behind to spread the Gospel, Yoda leaves Luke with the responsibility of sharing the Force. In each era, the Church must take up this missionary mandate for themselves. Yoda entreats Luke to "pass on what you have learned," just as we must do through evangelization. Yoda's final revelation that there is another Skywalker also applies to us. For Luke, he must find his living family member and share the Force with her. For us, we have a living family member in every other face on the planet, for we are all made in God's image and likeness. This also means we must practice the principles of Catholic Social Teaching while spreading the faith through evangelization.

Our Lightsaber

In myths, the hero-to-be is given a special tool along with special tutelage from a wise sage before going to meet his or her trials. For the Jedi the lightsaber is the tool, and tutelage comes from such sources as Obi-Wan and Yoda in the original trilogy, and the Jedi Order with its High Council in the prequels. For us, the tutelage comes from Christ, the Holy Spirit, Sacred Scripture, Sacred Tradition, and the wisdom of the Church with its Magisterium. The tools we have are abundant, but **I hope to have shown that the mythology of *Star Wars* is one more tool we may add to our belt in living and evangelizing the Catholic faith in contemporary society.**

Star Wars is the dominant myth of popular culture with many connections to the truths of Catholicism. We may use these similarities to speak with others hungry for the truth of the Gospel in a fun, enlightening, and non-threatening way. For example, if we saw someone wearing a Vader t-shirt, we could say, "Oh, Vader! I really appreciate how his self-sacrificial love reflects Christ and saves the galaxy, don't you?" Similarly, whomever we are with the next time we see merchandise or advertising for *Star Wars*, we might say, "I really enjoy the emphasis on faith in *Star Wars*," or, "Don't the Jedi remind you of Catholic priests?" *Star Wars* allows us to enjoy a good story, while addressing deep topics and powerful themes. Let us take advantage of this franchise for the greater glory of God. May the Lord be with you, always!

---

[1] Simon Beecroft and Pablo Hidalgo, *Star Wars Character Encyclopedia*, 2nd ed. (New York: DK Penguin Random House, 2016), 121.

[2] Ibid., 133.

[3] James Luceno, *Star Wars: Catalyst – A* Rogue One *Novel*, Audiobook narrated by Jonathan Davis (Random House Audio, 2016).

[4] Chuck Wendig, *Star Wars Aftermath: Empire's End*, Audiobook narrated by Marc Thompson (Random House Audio, 2017), 6:36:00.

[5] Joshua Hays, *A True Hope: Jedi Perils and the Way of Jesus* (Macon, GA: Smyth & Helwys, 2015), 53.

Bibliography

"40 Years of Star Wars Panel." Lucasfilm Ltd., Star Wars Celebration Orlando, 13 April 2017. https://www.youtube.com/watch?v=YI5QodTtlME (accessed 22 July 2017).

Anker, Roy M. *Catching Light: Looking for God in the Movies*. Grand Rapids, MI: William B. Eerdmans Publishing Company, 2004.

Barnes, Marc. "Rogue One and the Return of Reverence." *First Things*, 3 January 2017. https://www.firstthings.com/web-exclusives/2017/01/rogue-one-and-the-return-of-reverence (accessed 24 March 2017).

Barron, Robert. *Catholicism: A Journey to the Heart of the Faith*. New York: Image, 2011.

Beecroft, Simon and Pablo Hidalgo. *Star Wars Character Encyclopedia*. 2nd ed. New York: DK Penguin Random House, 2016.

Bortolin, Matthew. *The Dharma of Star Wars*. Somerville, MA: Wisdom Publications, 2015.

Campbell, Joseph. *The Hero with a Thousand Faces*. 3rd ed. Novato, CA: New World Library, 2008.

Carr, Fr. Robert J. "God's grace & Star Wars III." *Catholic Online*, 2005. http://www.catholic.org/featured/headline.php?ID=2247 (accessed 24 March 2017).

Catechism of the Catholic Church. 2d ed. Citta del Vaticano: Libreria Editrice Vaticana, 1997.

"Count Dooku." *Star Wars Databank*. http://www.starwars.com/databank/count-dooku (accessed 8 July 2017).

Dalton, Russell W. *Faith Journey Through Fantasy Lands: A Christian Dialogue with Harry Potter, Star Wars, and The Lord of the Rings*. Minneapolis: Augsburg Books, 2003.

Davies, Bess Twiston. "First School to Teach Jedi." *The Times* (London), 4 September 2004, 39.

Fitzpatrick, Sean. "Use the Force: A Catholic Strategy for Star Wars." *Catholic Exchange*, 21 December 2015. http://catholicexchange.com/use-the-force-a-catholic-strategy-for-star-wars (accessed 24 March 2017).

"Force Ghosts – The Lost Missions Q&A, Star Wars: The Clone Wars." Star Wars Youtube Channel. Published 4 December 2014. https://www.youtube.com/watch?v=iKWDZaxUoMg (accessed 26 July 2017).

"Force Planet." *Star Wars Databank*. http://www.starwars.com/databank/force-planet (accessed 27 July 2017).

"Force Priestesses." *Star Wars Databank.* http://www.starwars.com/databank/force-priestesses (accessed 27 July 2017).

"Force Priestesses – The Lost Missions Q&A, Star Wars: The Clone Wars." Star Wars Youtube Channel. Published 26 November 2014. https://www.youtube.com/watch?v=iKWDZaxUoMg (accessed 26 July 2017).

Golden, Christie. *Star Wars: Dark Disciple*. Audiobook narrated by Marc Thompson. Random House Audio, 2015.

Gordon, Andrew. "Star Wars: A Myth for Our Time." *Screening the Sacred: Religion, Myth, and Ideology in Popular American Film*. ed. Joel W. Martin and Conrad E. Ostwalt Jr. Boulder: Westview Press, 1995.

Gray, Claudia. *Star Wars: Bloodline*. Audiobook narrated by January LaVoy. Random House Audio, 2016.

Gray, Claudia. *Star Wars: Lost Stars*. Audiobook narrated by Pierce Cravens. Random House Audio, 2015.

Greene, Amanda. "Faith & the Force." *Star News*. Wilmington, NC, 21 May 2005, 1D, 4D.

Greydanus, Steven D. "Is 'Star Wars' Gnostic?" *National Catholic Register*, 29 December 2015. http://www.ncregister.com/daily-news/is-star-wars-gnostic (accessed 24 March 2017).

Grimes, Caleb. *Star Wars Jesus: A Spiritual Commentary on the Reality of the Force*. Enumclaw, WA: WinePress Publishing, 2007.

Guinness, Sir Alec. *A Positively Final Appearance: A Journal 1996-1998*. New York: Viking, 1999.

Hays, Joshua. *A True Hope: Jedi Perils and the Way of Jesus*. Macon, GA: Smyth & Helwys, 2015.

Hearne, Kevin. *Star Wars: Heir to the Jedi*. Audiobook narrated by Marc Thompson. Random House Audio, 2015.

Henderson, Mary. *Star Wars: The Magic of Myth*. New York: Bantam, 1997.

Hodge, Joel. "How 'Star Wars' Answers Our Biggest Religious Questions: The Movies Take on – and Subvert – Christian Themes." *The Washington Post*, 21 April 2015. https://www.washingtonpost.com/posteverything/wp/2015/04/21/how-star-wars-answers-our-biggest-religious-questions/?utm_term=.4de7970e2ea0 (accessed 24 March 2017).

Holy Bible, New American Bible. Wichita, KS: Fireside Bible Publishers, 1987.

John Paul II, Pope St. *Redemptoris Missio* (7 December 1990) http://w2.vatican.va/content/john-paul-ii/en/encyclicals/documents/hf_jp-ii_enc_07121990_redemptoris-missio.html (accessed 24 July 2017).

Johnston, E. K. *Star Wars: Ahsoka*. Audiobook narrated by Ashley Eckstein. Random House Audio, 2016.

Johnston, Jenifer. "Jedi, Our Fourth Religion Thanks to the Pagans." *The Sunday Herald*, 28 March 2004, 6.

Jones, Timothy Paul. *Finding God in a Galaxy Far, Far Away: A Spiritual Exploration of the Star Wars Saga.* Sisters, OR: Multnomah, 2005.

Kemp, Paul S. Star Wars: *Lords of the Sith.* Audiobook narrated by Jonathan Davis. Random House Audio, 2015.

Lesley, Alison. "How Obi-Wan Kenobi of 'Star Wars' Became a Devout Catholic." (14 December 2015). http://www.worldreligionnews.com/religion-news/christianity/how-obi-wan-kenobi-of-star-wars-became-a-devout-catholic (accessed 24 March 2017).

"List of References to Star Wars in Movies." *Star Wars Fanpedia.* http://starwarsfans.wikia.com/wiki/List_of_references_to_Star_Wars_in_movies (accessed 22 July 2017).

Luceno, James. *Star Wars: Catalyst – A Rogue One Novel.* Audiobook narrated by Jonathan Davis. Random House Audio, 2016.

Luceno, James. *Star Wars: Tarkin.* Audiobook narrated by Euan Morton. Random House Audio, 2014.

McDowell, John C. *The Gospel According to Star Wars: Faith, Hope, and the Force.* Louisville, Westminster John Knox Press, 2007.

Morrissey, Christopher S. "The Reality of Myth and the Force of Star Wars." *The Catholic World Report*, 19 December 2015. http://www.catholicworldreport.com/2015/12/19/the-reality-of-myth-and-the-force-of-star-wars/ (accessed 24 March 2017).

Moyers, Bill. *The Mythology of Star Wars with George Lucas and Bill Moyers*. Public Affairs Television, Inc., 1999. https://vimeo.com/groups/183185/videos/38026023 (accessed 21 July 2017).

Norton, Virginia. "Facing the Dark Side Final Installment of 'Star Wars' Presents Classic Struggle Between Good and Evil." *The Augusta Chronicle* (Georgia), 21 May 2005, D1.

Papandrea, James L. *From Star Wars to Superman: Christ Figures in Science Fiction and Superhero Films*. Manchester, NH: Sophia Institute Press, 2017.

Paul VI, Pope. *Evangelii Nuntiandi*. (8 December 1975) http://w2.vatican.va/content/paul-vi/en/apost_exhortations/documents/hf_p-vi_exh_19751208_evangelii-nuntiandi.html (accessed 25 October 2017).

Pinsky, Mark I. "Battle of All Faiths Builds Over Lessons of Star Wars Films." *Edmonton Journal* (Alberta), 4 June 2005, B13.

Porter, John M. *The Tao of Star Wars*. Atlanta: Brumby Holdings, Inc., 2003.

Rosen, Steven J. *The Jedi in the Lotus: Star Wars and the Hindu Tradition*. United Kingdom: Arktos Media Ltd., 2011.

Sansweet, Stephen J. *Star Wars Encyclopedia*. New York: Ballantine, 1998.

Skojec, Steve. "Star Wars: Catholic Ethos, Universal Appeal." *One Peter Five*, 17 December 2015. https://onepeterfive.com/star-wars-catholic-ethos-universal-appeal/ (accessed 24 March 2017).

"St. John Bosco." *Catholic Online.* http://www.catholic.org/saints/saint.php?saint_id=63 (accessed 24 July 2017).

Star Wars Empire of Dreams: The Story of the Star Wars Trilogy. DVD. Executive Produced and Directed by Ken Burns. Lucasfilm Ltd., 2004.

"Star Wars: Tarkin – Exclusive Excerpt!" http://www.starwars.com/news/star-wars-tarkin-exclusive-excerpt (accessed 7-7-17).

Staub, Dick. *Christian Wisdom of the Jedi Masters.* San Francisco: John Wiley & Sons, 2005.

Ultimate Star Wars. New York: DK Penguin Random House, 2015.

Wendig, Chuck. *Star Wars Aftermath.* Audiobook narrated by Marc Thompson. Penguin House Audio, 2015.

Wendig, Chuck. *Star Wars Aftermath: Empire's End.* Audiobook narrated by Marc Thompson. Random House Audio, 2017.

Wendig, Chuck. *Star Wars Aftermath: Life Debt.* Audiobook narrated by Marc Thompson. Random House Audio, 2016.

Wilkinson, David. *The Power of the Force: the Spirituality of the Star Wars Films.* Oxford: Lion, 2000.

About the Author

Anthony Digmann serves the Catholic Church as a speaker, author, and educator. He has appeared internationally on Catholic television and radio, such as EWTN and Radio Maria. In addition to *Using the Force: Star Wars and Catholicism*, Anthony is the author of *Sign of Contradiction: Contraception, Family Planning, & Catholicism*, as well as several articles published in diocesan periodicals across the country.

Anthony has a Master's degree in theology and has served the Church professionally in Catholic schools, parish ministry, and on councils of the Archdiocese of Dubuque since 2006. He is available to speak on a number of topics including: *Star Wars* and Catholicism, Catholic apologetics, evidence for God, Science & Theology, evidence for Christianity, demonology & exorcism, and the Church's teaching on contraception and family planning. Anthony lives with his family in Dyersville, Iowa, the home of the St. Francis Xavier Basilica and the Field of Dreams.

AnthonyDigmann.com

Made in the USA
Middletown, DE
26 December 2019